I0824256

GIORGIA'S VISION

GIORGIA MELONI
IN CONVERSATION WITH
ALESSANDRO SALLUSTI

TRANSLATED BY SYLVIA NOTINI

FOREWORD BY JD VANCE

Skyhorse Publishing

Skyhorse Publishing books may be purchased in bulk at special discounts for sales promotion, corporate gifts, fund-raising, or educational purposes. Special editions can also be created to specifications. For details, contact the Special Sales Department, Skyhorse Publishing, 307 Fifth Avenue, 4th Floor, New York, NY 10016 or info@skyhorsepublishing.com.

Visit our website at www.skyhorsepublishing.com.

Please follow our publisher Tony Lyons on Instagram @tonylyonsisuncertain.

10 9 8 7 6 5 4 3 2 1

Library of Congress Control Number: 2025941013

Cover design by David Ter-Avanesyan

Print ISBN: 978-1-5107-8358-4
Ebook ISBN: 978-1-5107-8359-1

Printed in the United States of America

Contents

Foreword

Europeans deserve good statesmen. Just as Americans should hope for enlightened leaders in our own country, we want voters across Europe to elect men and women who put their nations first—who defend their borders, promote the primacy of the family, and do not flinch at the sound of their own people's voices, even when they speak in dissent. We've seen the consequences when the opposite instead prevails: borders flung open to millions of migrants, surging crime and crumbling institutions, and a creeping sense among ordinary citizens that their leaders neither see nor serve them.

America wishes for good leaders in Europe not because of some paternalistic instinct over our friends across the Atlantic. We do so because the struggles Europe faces mirror the struggles we confront in the United States. In recent years, both our continents have been forced to reckon with questions about the fundamental nature of our societies. Foremost among them is whether a nation is merely a market, or whether it is a people—one united in shared cultural heritage, and a sense of duty both to the forebears who handed down the goods of civilization, as well as to the future generations set to someday inherit them.

For years, America has been a battleground for these debates. The left flank across Western politics would have us discard beliefs central to the functioning of our societies, like the dignity of the family, the authority of our laws and inviolability of our borders, and the importance of having a common culture. In Europe and North America both, it falls on the right to stand up to such nihilism. When conservatives fail to do so, or when we fail to stand for much beyond juicing short-term gains in the market, we see how easy it is to give ground to the Left. Global markets displace local workers. Authoritarian bureaucracies overrule parental rights. And throughout it all, the language of progress is used to conceal the hollowing-out of the things that give life meaning.

That is why the book before you matters. The conversations between Giorgia Meloni and Alessandro Sallusti vividly depict a leader willing to name the forces that undermine Western nations and, more importantly, offer a path forward to renewed greatness.

Meloni speaks of restoring Italy's "sense of community, without which we'll never be able to express our collective potential." It's the heart of her vision—a goal, I'll add, that's unmistakable to anyone lucky enough to have the opportunity to speak with her. Italy cannot thrive economically, she recognizes, until it has revitalized those institutions essential to any nation's wellbeing: family, faith, and love of country. Absent strong families and moral leadership, our markets become fragile, our civil institutions brittle. And, deprived of a common culture, future generations are left to inherit rootlessness and alienation.

Meloni's most perceptive and devastating diagnoses of the left center on its desire to upend the foundations of our civilization, and especially its willingness to weaponize mass migration in pursuit of that goal. She warns of a monstrous worldview in which "family, biological sex, national belonging, religious faith, every area that concerns one's identity has suddenly become a problem. . . . On the other hand, everything that dilutes is flaunted as though it were the new frontier of progress." In contrast, she identifies family as "the vital fabric of society . . . the place where generations hand down—via education, learning, and love—the history, traditions, and therefore the distinctive traits of a people." Meloni cites Pope Benedict XVI on the importance of recognizing the distinctiveness of our Western culture, and the arrogance it takes to presume all foreign peoples will share the values we choose to pass down to our children.

Most provocatively, Meloni suggests that leftists and other advocates of mass migration campaign to import migrants from cultures maximally alien to our own in order to erode workers' rights. "[T]he harder it is for you to integrate," she warns, "the more easily you'll accept precarious living conditions and work, inevitably creating a downward competitive spiral." It's an observation likely to resonate with American readers, who have seen the value of their own labor plummet when forced to compete with cheap foreign workers.

But even as Meloni calls for Italy to reassert control over its own sovereignty, nowhere does she suggest a retreat from the rest of the world. A strong Italy can stand in truer, more equal partnership with Brussels and its defensive allies; the same principle applies to a Europe more willing to increase its military spending and fulfills the terms of its treaty alliances. Americans should welcome that. A Europe that protects its borders, listens to its people, and revives its industrial base is a stronger partner in commerce and in security alike. The alternative—a Europe dependent on foreign energy and industry, unable to defend its own heritage, and eager to censor dissenting views—is bad for all of us.

Meloni's conversations with Sallusti amount to something much greater than a series of warnings, however. Together, they offer a blueprint for how to stabilize governance and return Italian society to a reflection of its people, rather than that of transnational elites. Reforming the tax code to attract investment and reward Italy's middle and working classes is one part of the plan. Making it easier to raise families and drastically reducing economic migration are others. Maybe unsurprisingly, these goals run parallel to what we're doing in the Trump administration. As in America, they're not small tasks, but it's vital for our nation's future that we succeed.

And as in America, success begins with listening to the people: what they convey at the ballot box, their thoughts and concerns, their hopes for the future. Meloni speaks of the Italian people not as subjects, nor as children who simply don't understand what's good for them. She plainly recognizes their aspirations, their frustrations, and most urgently their desire to feel pride in their nation. With a nod to some of her country's more historically neglected regions, she understands that Italy cannot thrive until all of Italy thrives.

Across the many hours of conversation in the pages to follow, one lesson consistently comes through: No one should underestimate the Italian people, nor the expectations they place in their leaders. Giorgia Meloni draws on that resilience to make the case that Italy's future must not be severed from its great history and that, for a nation to exert power abroad, it must first be strong at home. This should sound familiar to American readers, who hear arguments about our borders, culture, and the meaning of citizenship every single day. But for a generation in our own politics, there was no debate—only discussion confined to a cadre of likeminded elites, one that excluded divergent opinions held by millions of Americans, Republicans and Democrats alike.

That brings me to a final commonality between Giorgia Meloni and the populist politics of my own nation. There are few elected officials out there who would willingly spend hours of their time offering unfiltered thoughts to the world for public consumption. Fewer yet could offer the volume of thoughtful insights needed to fill an entire book. That Meloni can, and does, is ultimately what sets her apart from her contemporaries. Like the people she represents, she has something interesting and important to say. Those who would ignore her do so at their own peril.

JD Vance,
50th Vice President of the United States

Prologue

I meet her and say, "It's a pity that a Prime Minister can't consider writing a book to talk about her projects." She replies, "And why can't I?" Caught off-guard, I offer, "I'm not exactly sure—but there must be a reason if no one's ever done it."

"You should probably know," she replies, "that I'm not keen on doing what everyone else has already done."

Palazzo Chigi, late afternoon, the week before Christmas. Giorgia Meloni welcomes me for a quick exchange of greetings. I hadn't seen or heard from her in months—since last December, to be exact, when I moderated her debate at the Atreju Festival, the event that has grown to be the highlight of Italian politics—and not just for the Right. After that, we exchanged a few messages during the short, intense electoral campaign—not about politics or confidential matters, just thoughts we felt like sharing, for reasons we didn't entirely understand. Truth be told, I had seen her again, though only from a distance. She was onstage, and I was in the audience at the Brothers of Italy policy meeting held in Milan in April. The party had finally cleared the last hurdle. The atmosphere in that large hall at MiCo, Milan's convention center, felt electric. I remember returning to the office in time to draft the front page, and saying to my colleagues, "I don't know what you think, but I don't think the Brothers of Italy can be stopped." I could never have imagined the pace or the scale of the party's rise to power.

But let's return to that afternoon on Christmas Eve. Giorgia Meloni—Prime Minster Giorgia Meloni—has a fever, just like millions of other Italians. Unlike most, however, she can't afford even a moment's rest. She'll carry it with her for months, despite antibiotics and too many cigarettes. "How about a nice cup of hot tea?" she offers, slipping off her shoes and curling up on the three-seater sofa in her private office. I'm pleased—relieved even. I always worry about being an unwanted guest and never feel entirely at ease with those in power. That's why I tend to steer clear of Rome's palazzos, and why I'd only accepted this meeting as a pause in a calendar otherwise filled with much more important and demanding appointments. She tells me how she had the walls of this room painted pearl gray—the previous gold-colored damask tapestry clashed with the austerity of the time and the image that institutions should convey to those who enter there. She recounts the previous Prime Minister Mario Draghi's last piece of advice before he ultimately left the building, given with his trademark irony: always keep the windows overlooking the busy intersection of Largo Chigi shut "because there's so much smog, you'll get emphysema in just a few months." She admits that she doesn't feel fully at home in this building, once the residence of the Chigi banking family of Siena, which is far gloomier than one might expect. Meloni comments jokingly, "I don't get how someone could ever have lived in such a cold place." Though the remark soon gives way to more serious reflection. "At Palazzo Chigi, we breathe less solemnity than we do at Palazzo Montecitorio or Madama—let alone the Quirinale. And really, it makes sense. Everyone here has always been just passing through. In our legal system, the real power has always been elsewhere. It's as if these walls are whispering: 'Remember, you don't count for much—and you won't be here for long.'" As she says this, her gaze lifts toward the large, frescoed ceiling in her office—the famed Galleria Deti. There is an air of challenge here.

Inevitably, our conversation turns to the media—an institution we both know has not shown this Prime Minister the same benevolence it's extended to others in the past. She's amused, she says, by the daily, painstaking effort of certain newspapers—those that once depicted her as a harbinger of doom should she ever come to power—to now portray a version of Giorgia Meloni different from the one who once sat on the opposition benches. This, she believes, is an attempt to avoid acknowledging that they spent years attacking her, rather than reporting on her work and ideas. "To avoid admitting they didn't understand much—or that they'd waged a pointless psychological war to scare citizens—they now say *I've* changed. But then they screw up: in the same paper, one day I'm like Draghi, and the next I'm Mussolini. It's all very amusing.

"What they haven't grasped," she continues, "is that I will always only be myself. I've never imitated any model, neither past nor present. I do what I believe is right, nothing more. Even more amusing are those who clearly hate me but still offer daily advice on what I should do, whom I should be, what I should say—even which supporters I should seek. Oddly enough, this can come in handy. It's like they're inadvertently handing me a compass, showing me exactly what not to do, say, or become, and even which people to avoid. It also says a lot about the arrogance of the Left—and about a certain deep state that's connected to it—that can't rebuild its own identity, yet believes it can define the identity of the Right."

This reflection brings to mind her earlier words on a possible tell-all book. Something that can set the record straight, put things in the right order, with the kind of permanence that no article—only a book—could provide: "*It's a pity that a Prime Minister . . .*" And that, right there, is when I learned my lesson: never provoke Giorgia Meloni—whether for better or worse.

No sooner said than done. True to her style—quick, decisive, unflinching—meetings followed. A series of conversations at the end of busy days packed with state appointments, government meetings, cabinet meetings, and even missions abroad. One evening, she welcomes me without even having unpacked her bag, fresh from a trip to Kyiv, where she met with President Zelenskyy of Ukraine.

The clerks and security officers who police the corridors of Palazzo Chigi never quite understand why someone who isn't a staffer or official is coming to see her so often. After passing through all the security checks, I cross the courtyard of honor, which, on any ordinary day, dotted with parked cars, looks nothing like the solemn images Italians are used to seeing on the evening news. When the truly important guests arrive—those whose rank matches the Prime Minister's—they are welcomed with a red carpet, military bands and soldiers standing at attention. Beneath the entrance hall, there's an elevator with polished wooden walls, styled in the mid-twentieth-century aesthetic. Above it hangs a massive marble plaque commemorating Francesco Crispi, "the last hero of the Risorgimento, but the first in greatness," dated 1924. Upstairs, you pass through five large rooms, all roughly the same size, their walls bedecked with huge paintings and tapestries. They're almost always empty, arousing a quiet feeling of anxiety. You sense they only come to life during state visits or cabinet meetings. The famous round table used by ministers is just next door, on the same floor.

Finally, you arrive at the Prime Minister's office. It's not oval, like that famous one in Washington, DC, but rectangular. It's not particularly large, and it's more austere than you might expect. As you walk in, to the left is her desk, pushed against the long wall and facing a window. The desk is covered in pens of every kind and color—one of her passions that, according to friends, has become an obsession. At the back of the room, along the short wall, there's a small lounge area with a couch and two white upholstered armchairs.

That's where we spend entire evenings—sometimes late into the night, I with my recorder and notebook; she, sharing—subject after subject—her ideas, her vision, her projects, and her hopes.

The Path of Truth

Joan of Arc at Palazzo Chigi

Our first meeting was on a Sunday afternoon. After I was served a cup of coffee, we laid out the rules of engagement—starting with the matter of formality. "*Senta, presidente* . . ." I began, using the formal address in Italian.

"Alessandro, are you being formal with me?" she interrupted, surprised.

I explained that I thought it was appropriate for a series of interviews destined for a book—out of respect for the institution she represents. But she disagreed. "I don't like to pretend. We use the informal *tu* in everyday life, so we'll use it in the book, too."

This is going to be hard work, I thought.

And sure enough, she continued, "You're a journalist. By nature, you look for angles and emphasize things that will ignite political and media clashes. But that's not my goal here. I'm not looking for the kind of scoop you'd find in a newspaper. I want a book in which I can entrust my thoughts, tell the reader my point of view, the reasons behind the choices I've made—and those I will make. I want to lay out the vision that underlies these choices. I want to tell my truth and try to get others to reflect on it. I know what's going through your mind right now—that this book risks being terribly boring. But I intend to surprise you. In any case, that's what interests me. Do we agree?"

I tell her that we agree.

"Good, I trust you. Let's get started," she says.

* * *

Allow me to begin with what should really be the last question in this long conversation. What's your goal?

My biggest goal—or rather, the one that all the others depend on—is to give the Italian people back their pride in being Italian. To give them a state worthy of its great people, in which they can identify. An uphill task—and today, it seems impossible.

What do you mean when you say it's the goal on which all the others depend?

In the sense that no one can save this nation alone—it can only be saved if all of us believe in it. If each one of us, no matter the sector we might work in, decided that it's worth doing what they do not just for themselves or their loved ones, but also for the country. Restoring that sense of community, without which we'll never be able to express our collective potential in the best way possible. And to achieve that, the first step is restoring the credibility of our institutions. People need to trust them—because if you don't trust those who represent you, you stop trusting the very symbols of the state. And when that happens, you stop feeling any sense of belonging to them—and therefore to yourself. Put simply: you can write excellent laws, but if the state is perceived as the enemy, there will always be someone who gets around those laws. You can raise talented young people, but if the state doesn't value their skills, they'll emigrate to some other country, or give up believing that study, or competence, or value are what truly matter. Instead, they'll turn to short-cuts—knowing the right people, or following hollow role models who promise "minimum effort for maximum results." As I see it, there are no lasting results without great effort. The Romans said *per aspera ad astra*—through hardships to the stars. And in Italy, we can't keep pretending that's not how life is.

I dream of an Italy where the most "liked" influencers on social media aren't those flaunting a life of ease, with boats and luxury clothes, all bought with money they made by showing the world other boats and other clothes. I dream of an Italy of researchers who change the course of humankind, of soldiers who risk their lives to build peace, of doctors who perform miracles, of people who started from nothing but make history with passion and sacrifice. And I dream of the day when you can ask a young person what they want to be when they grow up, and they'll say: "I'm not setting limits for myself, but whatever I do, I want it to be something useful for my country."

A wishful thinker . . .

We'll see whether I'm a wishful thinker. But I'm definitely a dreamer. After all, I'm living proof that determination can lead you to do things you never expected. Would you have imagined that one day you'd be here talking to me—a forty-six-year-old right-wing woman from one of Rome's poorest quarters, held back by the system in every way possible—now sitting in this office on the second floor of Palazzo Chigi? Look around. Since 1961, this has been the seat of the Italian government, and it was here that people like Aldo Moro, Giulio Andreotti, Francesco Cossiga, Giovanni Spadolini, Bettino Craxi, Carlo Azeglio Ciampi, Romano Prodi, Silvio Berlusconi, Mario Monti, and Mario Draghi worked, to name just a few. People who—for better or worse—shaped Italian history. In short, did anyone ever seriously consider that what happened could actually happen? And that I could sit at this desk in this office?

Frankly, no. Some have compared you to Cinderella.

Fairy tales aren't real life. There are no fairies that can make you beautiful by waving a magic wand, nor are there princes who rouse you from sleep with a kiss. In real life, you have to pull yourself out of your own circumstances. That's what I've always believed and that's what I've always done—with the same determination I now bring to delivering what I promised Italians. And I owe it to them—because they're the ones who made it happen, not me. You see, when I became Prime Minister, I wasn't struck by the fact that many people were happy, but that they got so emotional. "Why are you all crying?" I asked with a mix of surprise and embarrassment. I even joked, "I haven't even started yet and you're already crying?"

But then I understood. My story breaks the taboos of a country at a standstill, of decisions over people's lives being made behind closed doors, the shattering of thresholds that we believe we are excluded from, of the idea that certain opportunities are beyond our reach. It wasn't just the political moment, the return of the Center Right to government, it was a government formed by the direct expression of a popular vote, after a decade of power games and governments chosen by the establishment. And there was something else in those strong emotions. I understood it completely when a very important person, sitting right here in the early hours of my term, explained his tearfulness in just a few words: "Giorgia, this wasn't supposed to happen." It's true. It may seem like a fairy tale, but it isn't. It's determination and sacrifice. Study, discipline—and obviously a good amount of luck. Though I'm not sure *lucky* is the right way to describe finding yourself governing Italy in this economic situation. But knowing that what seems impossible or like a fairy tale is actually within our reach can completely change people's way of thinking. All too often, I've heard people who didn't have everything they wanted say, "It's the government's fault," or "politics' fault," or "the fault of where I started." Sure, those things matter, and it's my job to work on that. But are we sure that's the only thing? What I mean to say, or ask is, "Are you sure you did everything you could to achieve the goals you set for yourself?" As I see it—and based on my personal experience—I'm certain that fate depends on what we are willing to do, on how much we're willing to work, on how much we're willing to sacrifice. Our fate depends on us. And if I can get this message across—while at the same time guaranteeing that everyone starts with the same conditions and the same opportunity to try—then we can change everything.

Right—meritocracy. It was the first controversy your government faced.

Unsurprisingly. The moment the Left heard that word, it flew into a rage. And do you know why? Because meritocracy dismantles the concept of the boss-state. It's what sets us free. You can't control it, you can't steer it. It doesn't need party affiliations or circuits that promote you based on your political loyalties—or rather, those you claim to have whenever it's convenient. Meritocracy is the opposite of real socialism and the Five Star Movement's principle that "one is equal to one." Because that's nonsense—no ifs, ands, or buts. It's been dragging us down since 1968. It pushed the idea that there's no point in giving it your all because everyone will get the same result anyway—even those who decide to do nothing. It's a shrewd way to move your friends up the line. One is not equal to one. One has to be equal to one when it comes to opportunities, not results, which instead depend on that one's subjectivity.

One of your mottos was: "Decline is not a fate, it is a choice."

It's the same principle I've been trying to explain all along, applied to an entire country. If someone who came from nothing can end up governing Italy, then maybe all of us can accomplish things once thought impossible. And if we can do it—and we are Italy—then this country, too, can reach goals we never imagined possible. That said, I'm not here to teach anyone anything. I just want to encourage people to believe in this idea because I know that the most efficient catalysts we have are willpower and optimism. And Italy desperately needs these right now because that's what we're missing. Not individual talent—we have that in abundance. Not creativity, not genius—ours are unique in the world and universally admired. Not determination, which we have, though these days we often reserve it for our private spheres than our public ones. Italians basically have everything.

Some of your fans have described this as the "Joan of Arc effect"—the story of a young woman deemed unfit for battle, yet who ends up leading the troops simply because she believes more than anyone else.

They say that because some of them like to point out that Joan of Arc was born on January 15—just like me. But let's not draw grand comparisons. What I did find amusing, though, was a book on horoscopes that described personalities based on their birthdates. Under January 15, it read: "The day of inevitable heroism." I relate to that—not the heroism part, just the inevitability. The truth is, I never set myself a personal goal to achieve, as many people rightly do. Instead, I've always given myself the goal of never sitting back and watching, but to act, to constantly expect more from myself. And maybe, in the end, that's what made the difference. Because, as Saint John Chrysostom said, "The Magi did not set out because they had seen the star, but they saw the star because they had already set out." I've always been on the move, and perhaps this perpetual motion made the opportunities I've seized feel almost inevitable.

Let's just say that, overall, you've been quite successful. Just to be clear—it's not flattery, it's a fact.

The way I see it, you either do something properly, or you don't do it at all. It's a principle I apply obsessively. Even something as simple as drawing with my daughter: I won't get up until I've finished—and that includes adding stars and a border. I've often been teased, even resented, for this obsessive approach—especially by those who have the misfortune of working with me. "Giorgia, we can't keep up with you," they say. But usually, they're the ones who end up doing things faster. I'm never the one slowing things down. Hard work, commitment, and responsibility can be contagious, but you can't lead a revolution if your team isn't on board. And only by inspiring an entire country can you create a revolution. That would be a tremendous achievement.

I see. But when you look around . . .

When you look around, Italy is envied, loved, and held in high esteem—everywhere except here. Here, the most influential figure seems to be Tafazzi, the legendary character created by the comedy trio Aldo, Giovanni, and Giacomo. Tafazzi was always criticizing the country's characteristics. We need to stop telling stories that end in failure because they simply aren't true. First, because the key economic and social indicators show the opposite. And second, because we still have a wealth of potential to harness. I understand that for the Left in opposition, it's convenient to say otherwise, but that's not the truth.

It's understandable that the Left isn't thrilled to see you here.

Naturally. And in fact, I consider their reaction perfectly normal—even if, as always, they lack a sense of proportion. And look, I'm not referring to what they say about me personally, but to what they say about Italy—especially abroad. We were in the opposition for many years, and we certainly didn't mince words, as is our right. But we had principles, the first being to act as a patriotic opposition party. That meant never speaking poorly of Italy abroad. Even before becoming Prime Minister, I was president of the European Conservatives and Reformists Party. Yet, I never once gave an interview to a foreign newspaper just to criticize the Italian government—because coming from me, it would have felt like an attack on Italy itself. The Left has never had that kind of restraint. They've always enjoyed leveraging their foreign friends to attack their Italian adversaries. Unfortunately, this behavior tends to be contagious, and we're seeing the effects: here, nothing ever seems good enough; everything other countries do is supposedly better than what we manage to do. We constantly cast ourselves as the ones lagging behind. This pessimism wears us down.

If we were even slightly more aware of our greatness—of how others truly see us—everything would change. A little healthy optimism would go a long way. That's why, for years, I've criticized the irresponsibility of those who use foreign platforms to attack their Italian rivals. And it's why I've urged the Left to play fair—without help from abroad—out of respect for the Italian people they represent. And it wasn't in vain. In my inaugural address, responding to those abroad who claimed they were "ready to monitor the rule of law in Italy" following my election, I said: "I think they can spend their time better. In our Parliament, we have competent and battle-hardened opposition forces more than capable of making themselves heard—without, I hope, outside help." It must have worked. Months later, when a French minister publicly criticized me and my government, both the Democratic Party and the Five Star Movement pushed back, saying in unison: "The Meloni government will be opposed by the Italian opposition—and no one else. We Italians are the only ones who have the right to say that this government is incapable of doing its job."

It was a small but significant victory.

Sir Winston Churchill, a great conservative politician, once said: "A pessimist sees the difficulty in every opportunity. An optimist sees the opportunity in every difficulty."

I agree. Unfortunately, here in Italy, pessimism often starts with the institutions themselves. This stems from what I mentioned earlier—political decisions that are frequently perceived by citizens as unfair, and often for good reason. That's why I believe we must be the first to set an example, and only then can we expect Italians to follow suit. Citizens shouldn't go easy on us—they should demand the best. If we can prove that we've done everything possible, then we have the right to ask them to do their part, too.

What do you mean by that?

I have always found it striking that Italy is the only country where the saying "Laws are made to be broken" is so widespread. Of course, laws are often incomprehensible, abstruse, even unjust—but this mindset risks extending far beyond the law. It's as if, in Italy, stealing from the state is somehow socially acceptable. And that's actually a stupid attitude because ultimately, we *are* the state. I was especially struck when Giuseppe Conte, defending himself against criticism that his so-called Superbonus renovation incentives had cost the state coffers billions of Euros, replied: "I said that the 100 percent Superbonus subsidy would be free for the families. I didn't say it was free for the state." As if the state didn't belong to its people. On the contrary, it is made up of Italians, funded by Italians, and it belongs to Italians. And if the state does something good, then it is fair to expect that it should not go to waste.

Let me give you an example. If I reduce tax on children's products by a certain percentage to help out families, then I expect—and, in fact, I demand—that the price of diapers or powdered milk also comes down.

If it doesn't, it means someone along that supply chain is ripping off the government and the consumers. In that case, even though I did something right and used public resources to do it, the Italian people wouldn't see the benefits because someone else exploited the system. It's true: Italy has a major problem with tax evasion. Our approach is to lower taxes and improve services, so that paying taxes is not seen as a rip-off but as a fair contribution to society. We need to start from the premise that if taxes are fair, more people will pay them. If that's not the case, then where would we stand?

Yes, where would we stand? That's my question to you.

Then we would have to accept that nothing will ever really change. But I don't believe that's what will happen. I've grown more and more convinced that I can trust the Italian people—and rarely has that belief been misplaced. I'm confident that every time we do the right thing, Italians will help us make it work as well as possible.

That's how you confront the person who says, "The state isn't for me."

Exactly—by leading through example. It's difficult for people to feel the state belongs to them if it acts in ways that defy common sense. But if the state behaves as they would have acted themselves, then they can feel that it is a part of them, and they are a part of it. It's important that Italians see a government that, admittedly, has its limits and may even make mistakes. But it does everything in its power to act in good faith, with humility and love. A government that isn't beholden to friends, lobbies, or powerful interests. One that doesn't seek approval at all costs, that doesn't exploit its citizens, and that has the courage to say when something simply can't be done—at least not at that moment or under those conditions. In short, I believe it is possible to rebuild a new relationship between the state and its citizens, one based on mutual trust. Trust is the foundation for any change.

Rebuilding a relationship with someone who has betrayed your trust can be done—but some say it's like patching up a torn outfit. The tear is still visible.

Then we should mend it with the thread of truth. Governing with honesty is fundamental. Those who haven't done so—and the list is long—have always paid a high price in the end. Lying or staying silent may be a shrewd choice in the short term, but it's foolish in the medium term. First, because lies never solve problems. Second, because the truth always comes out. And when it does, people realize that you tried to deceive them. It's better to tell people the truth and accept the criticism—from those who profit, from those who don't understand, or those who pretend not to. How often do parents have to make decisions their children don't understand and criticize them for? And yet, I've never seen a good parent change their mind about something that's truly in their child's best interest, just to avoid conflict. And let me be clear, I don't view Italians as children. I'll leave that paternalistic approach to others in politics. All I'm saying is that when you're in office and make decisions, you have access to a broader view of the situation—one that others aren't expected to have. And that can lead to decisions that aren't immediately comprehensible.

Let's talk about a word that politicians love: "change." It can be a double-edged sword in the sense that, in the end, you also risk changing your ideas. There's a sentence that stands out from your memoir, I Am Giorgia*: "In a world where everyone is trying to be someone, my goal is to remain true to myself, whatever the cost."*

I can confirm that: whatever the cost. You see, it kills me when I hear people say things like, "Meloni has changed her mind about everything—from excise duties to Europe." But that accusation doesn't make sense. If it were true, the Left would be delighted and sing my praises. Instead, they insult me even more than before. And do you know why? Because what we're actually proving is that you can govern without selling out. And that, for many, raises the idea that *they* have sold out. Of course, I can't say that outright—and I can't say that for ten years they talked about a version of the Right that didn't exist. So now, they need to claim that *I'm* the one who's changed.

Of course, I'm different—but not from who I was before. I'm different from how they portrayed me, both then and now. And now, you can see that. I've been saying the same things consistently, with the same conviction and the same pragmatism. I'll take this conversation as an opportunity to prove it. Do I use a different tone today? Absolutely. I'm the Prime Minister now, and that's a very different role from being the leader of the opposition. Let's put it this way: it's one thing to speak through a microphone with a powerful sound system; it's another to try to be heard by shouting in the middle of a noisy stadium. In short, the tools I have today are much more powerful—but my vision remains the same: firm and coherent.

Here's an example: in the past, I wasn't exactly a drilling enthusiast—we had enough gas and oil reserves, more than enough. But then one day Russia invaded Ukraine, and what happened happened. So now, if I have to choose between drilling and candlelight, I choose drilling, no question. The same goes for excise duties on gas. I've said it before and I'll say it again: they're too high and should be reduced as soon as public finances allow. But it simply isn't true—despite what the Left has tried to claim—that Brothers of Italy's election manifesto promised to cut excise duties. You just have to read it to know it's not true. Knowing full well the situation of the state coffers we were going to inherit, we put forward a realistic economic program—I'd say it was a very honest one. We pledged to neutralize the windfall state revenues received from high fuel costs, meaning that we wouldn't cash in on the price rises at the pump but instead reallocate the higher VAT earnings to reduce the duties paid. And that's exactly what we did when we came to power. We couldn't have done more—it's obvious that if you must spend tens of billions of euros in three months, creating more debt, to stop the rampant speculation on household and business bills, you don't have the money to cut excise duties in a structural way. I won't accept lessons on consistency from people who have happily crossed the whole political spectrum just to stay in government. Let the Left keep playing with words. I trust the people to look at the facts. And the facts don't lie.

Ultimately, consensus also comes from words.

In the short term, perhaps. In the long term, no. Of course, if you're weak, if you're struggling, if you don't have enough time to implement your projects—as has been the case for almost every Italian government—then anything goes. But that's not the situation for us, and I see that as our greatest strength. Have you noticed that in the eleven years between the end of 2011 and October 2022, we have had seven governments and six Prime Ministers? I'm not great with numbers, but the figures speak clearly: every eighteen months we have torn everything up and then started all over again—most of the time changing course entirely. By comparison, Angela Merkel governed Germany nonstop for sixteen years, from 2005 to 2021. Let's not forget that not one of those seven Italian governments had been chosen directly at the ballot box. The results? Zero credibility around the world, zero industrial strategy, decisions made in the interests of political parties rather than citizens. And we're still paying a very steep price for it.

So what do you see on the horizon?

Five years—and that's the only horizon that interests me.

No one in the history of the Republic has ever succeeded. Silvio Berlusconi came very close in the 2001–2006 legislature, but he fell at the last hurdle.

It's ironic that I might succeed precisely because I don't want to stay. Believe it or not, I see this phase of my life as a time of suspension. And, frankly, I can't say I'm happy or that I like it. I don't like living in a protective bubble; I don't like living as though I'm in a Big Brother house. I miss driving my car and turning up the volume to listen to my favorite songs. I miss being able to go out whenever I feel like it, to go jogging by myself. I miss—and this is something I've missed for many years now—being free to sit down in a café, have a cup of coffee, and read the newspaper without anyone recognizing and staring at me. Etched in my mind is a photograph of Pier Luigi Bersani sitting alone at a table and drinking a beer. I was struck by just how much that picture caused a stir. It captured a rare freedom that a well-known politician—and even more so, a Prime Minister—simply doesn't have.

I suffer from the loss of my normal life because, yes, I enjoy being a regular person, someone with an ordinary daily routine. A few months ago, at the start of my term, some friends invited me to lunch in Anzio for a birthday celebration. I rounded up my family, got my car, and joined them. To me, it was the most natural thing in the world. But good heavens! The security detail, inspectors, newspapers—everyone went crazy. How could a Prime Minister possibly just go out like that, without protection? And that's when I fully realized this great paradox: I made every decision in my life to be free, and now I find myself the least free person I know.

It's a famous syndrome, often called the "loneliness of the leader." Many of your colleagues suffer from it.

At first, the impact was hard. But then I found a philosophical explanation that helped me make sense of it all.

What's that?

Are you familiar with Gustave Thibon?

Gustave Thibon, the "peasant-philosopher." They called him that because of his humble background. As a Catholic, he spent the twentieth century engaged with the great French intellectuals.

Exactly. He said, "Being free is not about the extent to which we do not depend on anything or anyone; we are free to the extent to which we live off what we love, and we are slaves to the extent to which we depend on what we cannot love." So I, who love Italy more than anything else—after my daughter—am actually a free woman, even if I now have to make many personal sacrifices compared to before.

Right. But we still haven't solved the problem of consensus.

Consensus must be viewed over the medium term. I've seen leaders soar to the top and then vanish after two years. And I've seen others who have fought all their lives, with their popularity rising and falling, but who stayed steady and ultimately left a real mark. It explains itself. I believe that politics is divided into two categories: leaders and followers. Leaders are those who know how to point out a path, taking full responsibility, especially in difficult times. Followers are those who chase public moods, saying what people want to hear at that moment, without asking questions, to win instant consensus. I have no doubt which of the two is the real politician. But forging a path is harder—much harder—than following a mood. It requires a fair amount of awareness and patience.

Also because, unfortunately, the most important actions are the ones that create the least consensus. Here's a simple example: prevention.

A few months ago, I met with the families of the Rigopiano disaster victims. It was one of the most difficult, emotional days of my life. Not just because of the meeting itself, but because of a letter written by Gaia, an eleven-year-old girl who lost her mother in that ill-fated hotel buried by an avalanche. Gaia had her father deliver the letter to me. She wrote about how much she missed her mother every day, how she wished her mother could see her growing up, and how she demanded justice. When I turned the page and found the last picture she had taken with her mother, I confess, I cried my eyes out, alone in my office. Because this job brings powerful emotions, both good and bad.

The next day, I called Gaia to thank her for opening up to me. The families of the Rigopiano victims had vented their anger that the local administration lacked an avalanche emergency plan, the basis of the tragedy that had shattered their lives. The same was true for the elementary school collapse in San Giuliano di Puglia, where twenty-seven children and their teacher died, buried beneath the rubble of what remains one of the most terrible earthquake disasters in the history of our country. The school building also lacked the proper security certification. I could give countless other examples. Why? Why does this keep happening? I'll say it, and I take full responsibility for my words: it keeps happening because prevention does not create consensus. Governments that focus on preventing catastrophe will only incur economic and therefore political costs. They have to funnel away money from more conspicuous priorities. This is money that may prevent a catastrophe, but because nothing visibly happens, no one gives you credit for it. Instead, if you rush to the disaster site wearing a helmet, you create empathy and people shake your hand, saying, "Thank you for being here. Don't abandon us."

Several years ago, I read about Kōtoku Wamura, the mayor of a Japanese village who was harshly criticized by his people—even scorned—because of his "waste of public sources" that he had allotted for the construction of a major anti-tsunami barrier. Well, when the tsunami struck in 2011, that town was the only one spared. Today, his gravestone is a pilgrimage site for those who recognize him as a hero, and rightly so. He was one of those "silent heroes" described by Nassim Nicholas Taleb in *The Black Swan.*

What I want to say—to myself and others—is this: you must never be afraid of losing consensus if you're convinced that you're doing the right thing for your community. But it also means that you must have the strength and foresight, to never—never—make decisions based on the polls. Polls and screaming headlines must always be taken with a grain of salt. Recently, I read a headline in a major newspaper: "Meloni down, PD on the rise." When I read the whole article, I found that I'd lost 0.2 percent while they had gained 0.4 percent with a ten-point gap still in my favor and a three-point margin of error. So, what are we talking about?

In other words, if I believe something is right, I'll do it—even if it's not immediately understood, even if it might cost me politically. I shared the most intimate part of this phase of my life with Bruno Vespa, who interviewed me for his last book. My goal is not to be reelected in five years. I know that this might not happen—and that outcome would have both advantages and disadvantages. My goal is that when I die—whether in five years, twenty, or forty— someone I've never met puts a flower on my grave to thank me for what I did for Italy, like Mayor Wamura. Because true revolutions take time to be understood.

Going down in history, not just making headlines. That's ambitious...

I've often asked myself if I am ambitious. To be sure, I looked up the word in the dictionary: "An ardent desire for something; the desire to achieve a particular end." . . . Yes, I am ambitious. Because ambition in itself is good—it's the aim you pursue that defines whether it becomes something unhealthy. I want to make a difference in what I believe in and in what I love. I believe that what corrupts ambition, what makes it murky, is vanity—the most dangerous of the seven deadly sins. I learned this from *The Devil's Advocate*, the 1990s movie starring Keanu Reeves and Al

Pacino. It's a metaphor for the eternal battle between Good and Evil. In the movie, Evil—brilliantly portrayed by Al Pacino as the devil—seems defeated when Good, played by Keanu Reeves, withstands being corrupted by greed. It appears as though the movie is headed for a happy ending, when we see a good man refusing the help of the devil. But as we know, the devil comes in many forms. He turns into a reporter and approaches the good lawyer who rejected him, asking for an interview. Reeves considers this and agrees, leaving satisfied. The reporter turns back into the devil and says, "Vanity, definitely my favorite sin." Vanity is what ultimately betrays most human beings—and many politicians. I'm ambitious, but I'm not vain.

Preserving Who We Are

The Return of Identity

A few months before this meeting, I had been reading *Leadership* by Henry Kissinger, which had just come out in the Italian translation. In it, the grand old man of American politics describes some of the world leaders he had met. In the chapter dedicated to Margaret Thatcher, "The Strategy of Conviction," Kissinger, now one hundred years old, describes how surprised people across the ocean were in 1979, when they heard the news that Margaret Thatcher had become Prime Minister of the United Kingdom. I was particularly struck by one paragraph:

> Thatcher labored to cast off the shackles that had limited her predecessors—particularly the nostalgia for lost imperial glories and the abiding regret of national decline. . . . When she first took office, however, Thatcher's success was far from guaranteed; indeed, she was not expected to remain in power for long. Having wrested control of the Conservative Party from an exclusively male establishment that tolerated her under duress, she possessed only a meager share of political capital. Her previous record in government had been unremarkable; she had no great following in the country at large, and her experience in international

> relations was negligible. Not only was she Britain's first female prime minister, she was also at that time a rare Conservative leader drawn from the middle class. In nearly every way, she was a complete outsider.[1]

Margaret Thatcher was the first female Prime Minister, a conservative, an outsider, someone from the middle class who was looked down on with skepticism: when Giorgia Meloni, for whom all these same things can be said, was sworn in as Prime Minister, I took a picture of that page from the book and sent it to her on WhatsApp, accompanied by the eye-winking meme and the message: "Am I mistaken or is this about you?" A few minutes later, she replied: "I wish it were." Exactly: I wish.

President Meloni, what does the Right mean to you?
The Right is the field of reality.
As opposed to whom? To what?
To the utopias of the Left.
And what about fascism?

It has nothing to do with my field. And the same goes for every other authoritarian or totalitarian experience. I have always fought hard to uphold freedom. Freedom to vote, freedom to do business, freedom of expression. The nostalgia for a regime in our political setting only exists in the Left's imagination, which, if it didn't bring up that bugbear, would lose two-thirds of its reason to exist. In other words, because they no longer have an identity, they think they can solve the problem by hiding behind that of their forefathers. But politics makes sense if it acts in the present. This explains why people don't understand the Left and no longer feel represented by that party. Because today's problems cannot be solved by waving yesterday's flags. Besides, not even as concerns this

---

1 Henry Kissinger, *Leadership. Six Studies in World Strategy*, New York: Penguin Books, 2024, p. 323.

are they credible, even if we admit that these refined teachers of history have removed an important part of history, deleting completely from their memory the tragedies that the Communist dictatorships are responsible for. This is the difference between us and them. We have a grip on the past, they don't. They use history as a weapon with which to attack, and in the end, all they know how to do is look back. We use history as a tool that helps us to learn to look forward.

In, April 2022, at a party conference in Milan, you ended your talk with words about a vision . . .

Because politics simply cannot exist without a vision. Or rather, without a vision, politics is reduced to mere personal interests. When you do politics without being supported by beliefs, the only thing that remains is blind ambition as an end in itself. Getting to the top of the ladder so you can tell yourself that you were someone, cost what it may. But when you believe in something, then you know that you, and the roles you play, just like the political parties, are merely a tool to uphold those ideas. In the meeting in Milan, I was trying to express this concept when I said: "The only reason why we want to reach the top is so that we can look farther afield."

And now that you've reached the top, what do you see?

Unfortunately, I have an even better view of everything that doesn't work. In Italy, in Europe, in a West that is willing to give up its soul and sell off its values to the highest bidder. All things considered, the latter is the most important battle of our time.

But we are the West, that's a fact.

Yes, and another fact is that that the West seems to be doing everything it can to cancel itself. But identity is the first reality. What I am is real. And because what I am is the result of what generated me, of the traditions and culture I inherited, of the influence of religion in my civilization, all this, too, is the field of what is real. If you deny this for the sole purpose of putting a straitjacket on your desires, your whims, your interests, in other words, on your ideology, you end up no longer knowing who you are, so that you can live in a world filled with contradictions, so that you can pursue the impossible and deny the possible. You end up being a slave to that ideology.

Identity versus globalism?

The conflict is on both sides: on the one hand, the conservatives, that is, us, who defend the person with their identity because we know that that is the precondition for defending the rights of that person. On the other, the so-called progressives, but I would actually call them globalists, who pit a person against their identity, apparently to make them freer, but in practice to make them more unaware, and therefore at the mercy of those who are in charge.

Canceling identity to the advantage of whom?

That question would require a very complex answer. I will try to simplify. There are huge, immense economic concentrations that have a great influence, even more than that of many countries whose GDP is less than their revenues and who see identity as an obstacle to their power to concentrate wealth. We're talking about state-owned companies that, by not having territories and borders, need to standardize the customs and traditions and make them transnational if they are to survive. For them, identity is a limit.

Objection: Freedom to conduct business in a free market exists.

I know that, it's called "liberal democracy," and it's in our DNA. I certainly don't want to stop that. It's entirely legitimate, and I am well aware that thanks to that millions of people can more easily access goods and services. I am certainly not thinking about an economic model founded on autarky, and even less so about the demonization of wealth. What I'm saying is that within a free market we also need to protect the economic identities that, even though they are outside of the great concentrations, represent an asset. The issue of the Made in Italy brand comes to mind. What I mean, just to mention a case that has recently stirred up a great deal of debate, is how the hell could anyone want to impose a label on wine that says, "Warning, may be harmful to your health," and then subsidize the multinationals of synthetic meat or flour made from insects? Are we afraid to say that it's not wine that's harmful to your health, but its abuse, which, like all forms of abuse, causes problems? Let's talk about oil, another apt example. The French are pushing for Europe to adopt what's known as the *nutri-score*, a label on products owned by one of their companies: green for healthy ones, red for unhealthy ones. That said, our extra-virgin olive oil would get a red label based on the absurd idea that it contains too many saturated fats per liter. This is nonsense because no one would ever gulp down a liter of oil a day. Don't these distinguished scientists know that the first thing every nutritionist says is not to eliminate extra-virgin oil because, taken in the right amounts, it has many benefits? On the other hand, carbonated beverages produced in a lab get a green label because they contain no saturated fats. I'm amazed that this push comes from France, which competes with us for first place when it comes to denominations of origin, and instead seems to favor the reasons put forward by its large-scale distributors rather than those of its producers. I hope they change their mind. In the meantime, our opposition is total. In any case, to stay on the same subject, there is currently an attempt to reach a standardization of nutrition to the advantage of those who get rich with the quantity of the product sold rather than its quality. My belief, for instance, is that policies must support the healthy competition between Italian and French wines and cheeses, and not, on the contrary, favor those who would like to control and limit their spread in order to dominate, in another way, the food supply chain. This is my idea of a free market, in every sector: there cannot be a free market if there are laws that alter competition.

Will the Left be an accomplice to this design?

The Left will more than anything else be the foolish slave to this scheme because it doesn't want to come to terms with the fact that it was mistaken when it sold globalization like a sort of "invisible hand" that was going to distribute wealth and democratize less democratic systems. Clearly, that's not exactly how things went. Actually, what happened was the exact opposite.

And what did happen?

Thanks, so to speak, to free commerce without rules or safeguards, countries less democratic than ours got rich and earned a free rein in the world, but they are still backward when it comes to rights; see Russia and China. It must mean something if during this period both Putin and Xi Jinping—who have both had their advantages from globalization—both abolished the rule of a limit on the presidency, practically making it possible for them to stay in office for as long as they want to, and therefore going backward rather than forward. And there has been no redistribution of wealth. Quite the opposite. Wealth has become verticalized: the number of poor people grows, the middle-class risks disappearing, millions of people are just above the poverty level, and the rich are becoming fewer in number and more and more wealthy. This was the economic and social masterstroke, in other words, the disaster, that the Left participated in, or that, at best, it did not oppose, as I have just said, because of its ideological bias, or based on a political calculation.

So, what you're telling is that there is a plan underway to change society.

It's the other face of the do-gooder medal, a monstrous one: family, biological sex, national belonging, religious faith, every area that concerns one's identity has suddenly become a problem. Everything that defines you, that says who you are, is an enemy to be defeated. On the other hand, everything that dilutes is flaunted as though it were the new frontier of progress. That's a fact. Look, I was struck by all the debate about what Agriculture Minister Lollobrigida had said concerning wanting to defend Italian society from the risk of an ethnic replacement. Heaven forbid! They said his theories were supremacist, Neo-Nazi, and, of course, racist. Except that something doesn't quite add up.

What's that?

That ethnicity and race are two words that mean very different things. Let's take a look at what the Treccani Italian dictionary says:

> Race: In physical anthropology in the nineteenth century and the early twentieth century, major groupings of humankind that present distinct physical features (skin color, type of hair, shape of the face, the nose, the eyes, etc.) regardless of their nationality,

> language, traditions (for instance, white, yellow, black race; Australian, Sudanese, Nilotic, etc.).

Under the word *ethnicity* we instead read: "In ethnology and anthropology, human grouping based on cultural and linguistic traits." Race is what we are physically, ethnicity is what we are culturally. Well, either one or the other: either all those who pulled their hair out should revise their schoolbooks, or, in their opinion, we should be ashamed to insist on the fact that we want to defend our cultural identity. But, in this case, they should go all the way, and explain to the Italians that they consider it a good thing to replace their language and their culture. Then we can certainly discuss whether it's appropriate to use that expression but not because of the meaning in itself; only because the definition of ethnic replacement is one of those cases in which the Left has succeeded in winning the war of the words.

What exactly do you mean by that?

In every cultural battle we wage, the most lethal weapon at our disposal is the meaning we attribute to words. It doesn't matter what the word means, what matters is what you want it to mean. The idea that revolves around that word. If you manage to win that fight, you're already halfway there. The Left is historically better equipped in this because it has an army of people ready to repeat the concept that it wants to impose like a mantra, and because around our parts there has often been a sort of psychological subjugation that has made us sheepish. The case of ethnic replacement is one of these. Once you have succeeded in juxtaposing the word *race* with the word *ethnicity*, even though, as we saw before, they are two very different things, then you have obtained a concept that is perfectly acceptable like that of wanting to defend the identity of your people which becomes overlapped with the ridiculous idea of the superiority of one race over another. Arguing in defense of what you wanted to say becomes nearly impossible because you are overwhelmed by a wave of single-minded thinking, and in many cases, you find you are forced to let the concept go.

So, the battle has already been lost?

No, it's a battle that must be fought, also because if we lose this one it will be very hard to win the war. But often it's enough to circumvent the enemy, and it's easy for someone who has a large vocabulary, and the Italian language has a highly articulated vocabulary. I have never given up saying what I wanted to say. And in the end, we too, in the battle of the words, have had our victories. Think of the word *patriot*. When, at the Brothers of Italy meeting in Trieste, we used the title "Appeal to the Patriots," everyone made fun of us saying that we were nostalgic for the Risorgimento, that we were old-timers. Today, the parties compete to see who's the most patriotic of them all.

The Left has often won the war of words when it comes to immigration, isn't that so?

Probably. But then what was said was overwhelmed by facts and certain concepts no longer got across. Take the tragedy of Cutro. They tried to use it against the government, but even a person with the memory of a warthog [*the warthog is an animal with a very short memory span: it's known for scampering off when it sees a predator and then stopping in its tracks because it can't remember why it was running, she explains to me*] can remember that we have had similar tragedies in the Central Mediterranean with governments of all kinds, and almost always with the Far Left involved, for a total—according to the International Organization for Migrations—of over 26,000 dead or lost in ten years. That's when we realize just how immoral and cowardly the charges, both political and personal, that were leveled against me and the government after that tragedy were. The point is that we can keep on fighting as much as we want but if we don't understand that the only way to stop the deaths is to stop the trafficking, then people will continue to die. They can carry on with their sideshow hypocrisy, but anyone who is the least bit honest cannot actually believe that if I were to find myself at the site of the tragedy I'd just stand there and do nothing. If there were a shipwreck, I'd be the first to dive into the water to try to save a child, regardless of where they are from. Is there anyone who really believes, in their heart of hearts, that the government could possibly have given the order to not save those migrants, and that the state rescue workers who each and every day risk their lives to save others, would have complied with such a horrendous order? Of course not. And, as I said in Parliament, these people don't realize that by attacking the government they end up making the country look bad in general, casting a shadow over those who instead continue to do their best, often surrounded by the indifference of all the others, to save people. That said, the idea that we can go on this way, with the migratory flows continuing to grow, truly does pose a risk for the migrants' lives. Because whether you like it or not, there will always be something that can go wrong, a warning signal that isn't received, shipwrecked people who can't be reached. The only way to stop the trafficking is to fight illegal migration and manage the flows of legal migration, safely. That way we can also guarantee that those who arrive here have the dignified life they were hoping to have.

Easier said than done.

Right. It's a huge task because we are in a situation that has never been this complex before. There's a war that's wreaking havoc everywhere, including making the food crisis worse in Africa. Libya is still divided and Tunisia is at risk of collapsing. Wagner's mercenaries are destabilizing the Sahel, and fundamentalism is gaining traction. And in the midst of all this we also have to come to terms with a paralyzing ideological approach in place of a pragmatic one. The famous theory of "all are welcome" regardless of methods, criteria, and needs. But that's not my theory. To my mind, it should be managed quite differently. Are you a refugee who needs protection? Then we need to find a way to protect you. You're not a refugee, and you want to come and work in Europe? You are welcome to do so, but you must be compatible with the real possibility of intersecting your aspiration with our possibilities and needs, otherwise it'll be social chaos as well as human decline. This doesn't seem to me to be a racist theory; rather, it's the exact opposite.

The famous quotas.

Exactly. It's going to take time but we'll get there eventually. Because I know that when it comes to this issue it looks like the government isn't getting results, that some of those who supported us are starting to doubt our seriousness. But I prefer to pay the consequences now to be able to build structural solutions, rather than put forward propagandistic measures that are not a stable solution. To deal with the question in a definitive way, we especially need to work at an international level, and everyone knows I've been dedicating my time to this every single day. I often hear it said, by the opposition but not just them, that "you were supposed to enforce a naval blockade and then everyone saw it was impossible, just like we said it would be." A message that's easy to get out there, but inaccurate. Of course, it can be done, and that's what I'm working on. I have always talked about a European mission in agreement with the North African authorities to stop the departures, to open hotspots in Africa, to distinguish refugees from economic migrants, to distribute refugees throughout the twenty-seven countries in the European Union. And as concerns the economic migrants, we need to respond with training and investments so that Africa is in the condition of being able to prosper thanks to its immense riches. I agree with Pope Francis, who in his message on the 109th World Day of Migrants and Refugees said that: "Joint efforts are needed by individual countries and the international community to ensure that all enjoy the right not to be forced to emigrate, in other words, the chance to live in peace and with dignity in one's own country." When I discuss with Europe the "cooperation with countries of origin and transit," or "external dimension," when I work on the "Mattei Plan for Africa," when I bring investments to Libya, Algeria, Ethiopia, when I try to convince the international community to release the resources for Tunisia while I am at the same time working with the EU on a new partnership like the one we signed, what do you think I'm doing? Exactly that. It's very hard work that takes time, but in the long term, I'm optimistic about achieving my goals. Before this adventure ends, we will have put an end to the problem of illegal mass immigration.

Should it ever happen, the Left will have to pay you its compliments.

That will never happen, obviously. For them it would be a tragedy. Because illegal mass immigration is one of the principal tools of the war against identity. It should come as no surprise that the Left's pro-immigration campaigns are exclusively addressed to an extra-European immigration, when even in Europe there are people who live in poverty that can be compared to that of many Africans. Did you know that Moldova, for instance, has a per capita income that is less than that of most of the North African countries? And yet I haven't noticed anyone tearing their hair out in despair to favor Moldovan immigration. Have you ever wondered why? Because Moldavans, who are European, are too close to our culture. This means that they are not functional to the design of the so-called melting pot, that is, mixing as much as possible in order to dilute. That is much more functional to the design of the African migrant. And little does it matter whether the African or Middle Eastern or Central and Southern Asian migrant risks being integrated with greater difficulty. Because, here too, there's a possible hidden benefit for the large economic concentrations: the harder it is for you to integrate, the more easily you'll accept precarious living conditions and work, inevitably creating a downward competitive spiral. To sum up, this is the question I want to ask: Could it be that those who push for mass and uncontrolled migration only from certain parts of the world have two ulterior motives: to weaken the identity of the nations and to cut back on worker rights? And what does all this have to do with the highly acclaimed "solidarity"?

Compatible immigration, the old theory of a great Catholic intellectual, Cardinal Giacomo Biffi of Bologna, who was opposed by the progressive Church until the day he died. But what do the workers have to do with it?

They have a lot to do with it. Chaotically as well as illegally introducing masses of immigrants into the work system produces a generalized reduction in social and economic rights. The Left repeats the same mantra over and over again: "We need immigrants because they're willing to do the jobs that Italians aren't." Which isn't true. The truth of the matter is that immigrants are forced to accept jobs with terrible conditions, jobs that Italians are still in the position of being able to refuse. It's a sort of evolution of the slavery that was defeated centuries ago. Society's economic downward leveling out is also a consequence of the open doors policies, and it is always to the advantage of the same, few, schemers. You see, I wanted to put a stop to this. Is this a policy from the Right? Yes, we are in the field that coincides with that of common sense. The Italians elected me to do this and I will try to make it happen, whether George Soros or those who represent him like it or not.

Whenever we talk about the great financial powers that push for immigration, we inevitably end up talking about George Soros . . . is he the great puppet master?

I don't want to make it sound personal, also because as soon as you say George Soros, people on the Left start shouting starting from accusing us of conspiracy theories, and ending with much more serious insinuations. I don't believe in puppet masters, but when we talk about Soros, we're talking about someone who, in 1992, publicly claimed he speculated against the Italian lira, and who today, thanks to his galaxy of foundations, openly pursues a political agenda. This includes the generous funds given to some of the NGOs that deal with immigration. Similarly, he also intervenes in the political dynamics of certain countries. This also happened in Italy when, at the most recent political elections, he openly funded one party currently in the opposition with the manifest intention to stop the Italian Right. These are facts. Evidently, he considers me to be a political adversary. I simply acknowledge this without spiting those on the Left who describe him as a selfless philanthropist. I say it without acrimony and without any conspiracy thinking, upholding the freedom—you will allow me—to not agree with those who legitimately believe in a world without borders and without identity. I, just as legitimately, will fight for the exact opposite.

On many occasions, you've said that the right wing you have in mind must start from the family. My question to you is this: What does the family have to do with the destabilizing shenanigans that are going on around Europe?

The family is the heart of the problem, to the extent that it is the institution that is most of all in jeopardy. For centuries, we have said: the family, understood as the union between a man and a woman in a pact of absolute solidarity, is the vital fabric of society. The reason for this is obvious: it is only from the union between a man and a woman that children can come into the world naturally, children who are the vital lymph without which a community is destined to become physically extinct and even before that economically extinct because it means that there will be no future workers, who are the only real creators of wealth, without whom no state could remain standing. But not just that: the family is also the place where generations hand down—via education, learning, and love—the history, traditions, and therefore the distinctive traits of a people. The unraveling of the family will only lead to the unraveling of society overall. If we follow the Left, then we are nationalizing the family institution: the names Mother and Father, gone, the sexual identity of one's children, gone, educational rules percolating top-down and imposed by law, the selective cancellation of history—what is known as *cancel culture*—of all that is not functional to the new single-minded thinking, so that monuments are torn down, books are rewritten, movies are censored, even children's traditional fairy tales must be modified so they fit the new course. And do you know what skeleton key they used to do this?

No, tell me.

The mainstay of the family: the woman.

It would seem like the opposite is true: never before has the woman been protected like today.

Exactly. Precisely because the rights of women have grown and been consolidated over time, they are now sought after. If you think of it, gender theories taken to an extreme don't offer us a neutral model, but a male model. Even when it comes to the methods of assisted conception there can be up to five mothers, while the father is always one. It is the woman who is under attack, especially since she is a potential mother. Because motherhood is the core of every deep relationship. It is in the relationship between a mother and her child that we sublimate the sacrifice for the other, the unselfish care, the acceptance of imperfection. It is in the mother-child relationship that we learn to be a couple, to depend on each other, to love. If this cornerstone is destroyed, then we will just be monads, devoid of a relationship. The mother-child relationship holds the core of the relationship between human beings. And, think about this, if you believe that everything is related: we say "motherland" because the country is the mother and the person who is born there is indissolubly linked to it regardless of where they live. This obviously does not mean that a woman who chooses not to have children, or who can't have any, has something to feel guilty about. I myself had my only child, a daughter, at the age of thirty-nine, even though now I wish I had had her much earlier. Choices are individual and must be respected, but society, politics must preserve the most precious things we have. This means that those who would like it to be possible to buy children, to choose them from a catalog, to reject them if they don't fulfill their expectations, don't understand the kind of world they are contributing to imposing. This is why we will continue our battle against surrogacy, a dreadful practice that hides another new slavery involving women who are mostly poor. I've never heard of a rich, progressive, liberated woman lending her uterus to her maid or to some stranger. I wonder why it's always the opposite. Is this the model of emancipation of the kind of woman that the Left leans toward? Well, it's not mine.

But a person's sex drive and orientation are indisputably private.

Of course they are. I'm not talking about what happens in a personal relationship where people do what they want to. I'm talking about what goes on in parliaments, where lawmakers think they can enter a person's bedroom and lay down the law on what they do there. Or campaigns in which six-year-old children are told what homosexuality is while they exchange clothes with children of the opposite sex. Personally, I still believe in the rule that encouraged our school system to not talk about sexuality in schools, considering, rightly so, that the subject, at least for the younger ones, should be dealt with by the family. But the problem is that in Italy, and not just in Italy, we cannot talk about these subjects calmly. Either you uncritically agree with their, often bizarre, beliefs, or you are automatically added to the list of despicable homophobes.

Is there a problem of homophobia in Italy?

Homophobia, the discrimination against, aversion to, or fear of those who have a certain sexual orientation that can even lead to discrimination and even violence is an unacceptable scourge and must be fought against hard. But if you say that someone who doesn't think like you is a homophobe, if you say that a homosexual who doesn't agree with your ideas is a homophobe, then we are in another place completely. And, allow me to add, if you do it, you won't be of any help in fighting homophobia. I'm called a homophobe without actually being one, just because I fight against surrogacy and I don't agree that homosexuals should be able to adopt children, for reasons that I have already explained and that concern the rights of children to be able to depend on a father and a mother. Some homosexuals have used insulting, threatening tones with me; if I had done that to them, I would have been asked to stand down immediately. And yet I am the one accused of being a hater, even though in my entire life I have never been disrespectful of homosexuals. In one of the last Pride parades I saw a video of a comedienne who said I should "give my daughter away" because she was born out of wedlock and, obviously, "shut my mouth." Everyone applauded enthusiastically, those who fight against hate culture. But as long as I'm the target it's okay. Did you see what happened to poor Arisa? *[Translator's note: Arisa is an Italian singer and actress.]* Forever a champion of the rights of homosexuals, she had the courage to say, in an interview, that she thought I was brave and that she would have liked to convince me about homosexuals' rights. Good God! She was forced to forgo the Gay Pride event where she was supposed to perform. And the insults didn't end there. Isn't that discrimination too? Throwing out an artist who has always defended you in good faith just because she says she doesn't hate me? It made me sad to think that Arisa had to go through all this because of me.

Do you really think you can convince young people, who are dependent on social media, one of the most powerful tools in the hands of those who would like this new ethical order, of the value of your ideas?

Here we enter a crucial field, which is that of information, a word that has little to do with the brainwashing that is underway. You see, young people complain, and rightly so, that they're not taken into consideration. There's nothing new about that, it's always been that way, but today it's even more true. This is because adults are becoming less interested in belonging to a family, to a nation; historically, these are the drivers of one's future orientation and sense of responsibility. If you're not close to your family, if you don't feel the value of your country, then what does it matter what comes after you? If the past, that is, your roots, no longer count, if only the indistinct and selfish present of adults counts, adults who claim their rights but avoid their responsibilities, then what are we leaving for the future? That's why for the first time the younger generation feels abandoned. But I'm still an optimist.

It doesn't sound like it.

Look at my experience. I mean the experience of a modern and conservative Right. We won the elections also because we insisted on these issues despite the obsessively and massively aggressive media campaign against us. Unlike our rivals, and what our rivals say, we never used mean tones, we never disseminated hatred or discriminated against anyone. We explained what our ideas are and because—unlike theirs—they are reasonable ones, the people, including young people—I would venture to say especially young people—listened to us, and then voted. This is proof that a lie told over and over again doesn't always become truth.

Everyone wonders: "Fine, but how long will this credit line last?"

You mean the honeymoon? I'm not going to fall for that. You need to stay calm, cool, and collected. Politics is like a game of chess. Before you make a move, you have to figure out what's going to happen, envisage the next ten moves to be certain of where you'll end up. Of course, things can go wrong, lots of things can go wrong, but it's silly to do things in a hurry or because you're anxious. Haste and anxiety are two bad advisers. I'm not praising slowness, I'm praising efficiency.

Our Europe

The European Union Must Not Be an Exclusive Club

This time, the meeting isn't at Palazzo Chigi, but at a friend's house just outside Rome—one of the places where Giorgia Meloni occasionally takes refuge when her partner, Andrea Giambruno, is in Milan hosting his afternoon program on Mediaset.

She arrives for dinner: no police sirens, no flashing lights, just a small, discreet security detail—one she would gladly forgo if it weren't required by law (and by common sense, I might add). She stubbornly resisted having a security detail for years, ignoring the pleas of her friends, police chiefs, and prefects—until the day she became Prime Minister.

Her six-year-old daughter, Ginevra, is here, too. For her, it's a special day. This morning, her mother took her to school; tonight, they are still together. It's not an everyday occurrence, and Ginevra seems eager to express her joy by performing an endless series of perfect somersaults and pirouettes on the living room floor. Her mother watches her with pride and jokes, "Luckily, she has her father's physique." Then she cuddles her on the sofa, just like any other mother in the world would. Although Christmas has already passed, a few slices of panettone are served—"my favorite aperitif," Meloni says. Ginevra rushes off to play with a castle of fairies and princesses in the corner of the spacious room. "We leave it here," her mother explains, "because if we took it to our house, we'd have to find another place to live." As we wait for dinner, we switch on the recorder placed on the set dining table. Meloni has taken off the formal clothes of the Prime Minister and is now wearing a sweatshirt, pants, and white sneakers. The conversation turns to Europe, a topic once again dominating the headlines due to disagreements between Brussels and Rome—a familiar story.

"Let's be clear," she says. "Italy leaving Europe is not on the table. We are Europe—more than two thousand years ago, everything was born right here. It should come as no surprise that we were among the founders of the European Community. Without Italy, there would be no European Union."

And yet you have often been portrayed as leading the anti-European movement.

That narrative is false and biased. It's designed to scare people—to stop conservatives from gaining power and allow the Left to remain comfortably unchallenged at the center of the field. I completely distance myself from that.

Please, go ahead.

Europe is the cradle of the West. And what is the West? Let's simplify it as much as we can: the West is everything that Ancient Greece protected by establishing a frontier—a space within which, era after era, the foundational principles of who we are were shaped and then consolidated—and not without difficulty. Principles like freedom and equality of human beings. But also principles like the inseparable bond between faith and reason—a legacy of Christianity—that sets us apart from other cultures and religions. Pope Benedict XVI expressed this perfectly in his famous Regensburg address, which was, unsurprisingly, opposed by those who deny the centrality of Western culture. We Westerners tend to see our values—freedom, equality, democracy, individual rights, and the meeting point between reason and transcendence—as universal. But if we look around us, we have to admit that these are not universal values. They are characteristic of the culture of a specific part of the world.

It is our identity as Europeans and Westerners, as heirs to classical and Judeo-Christian culture. This is what the Conservatives have always sought to defend. Our critique of the European Union stems from the belief that Europe should not be reduced to an aseptic, supranational organization—a sort of exclusive club that one can only join with the right credentials and be thrown out of if other members disapprove. But Europe is far more than rules and labels. It's a shared history among peoples. It's the desire to build a common future. My criticism of the European Union arises from the desire to defend these cornerstones—in a word, identity—from an approach that can sometimes be too invasive and self-referential. In other words, I don't want to distance myself from Europe. On the contrary, I don't want Europe to distance itself from its own roots. That's why I fight those in Europe who deny who we are and work hard to weaken our identity.

So, you're saying you're a staunch pro-European.

When it comes down to the facts, yes—much more than many of those self-proclaimed pro-Europeans.

But a collection of sovereignties will never lead to a cohesive Union.

True, but that's not the right way to frame the issue. The real choice is not between being pro-sovereignty and being pro-European, as some like to suggest, only to fuel division.

Then what is the real alternative?

It's between a federation and a confederation.

You're playing with words.

Let me explain, then . . . We need to be very clear on this—because even on these issues, there's a war of words that risks playing into the hands of the Left. Today, those who are widely labeled in the dominant narrative as pro-European are, in fact, European federalists—supporters of a model in which the individual member states gradually lose their sovereignty, concentrating power increasingly in Brussels. So, if you look closely, the term *federalism* applied to the European community model actually encapsulates an idea that is diametrically opposed to the one we have about *federalism* in Italy. For us, federalism refers to the devolution of power from the center toward the peripheries—for example, from the state to the regions. In Europe, however, federalism means the devolution of power from the periphery to the center—for instance, from the national states to the commission. Strictly speaking, those who advocate for this model shouldn't be called *federalists* but *European centralists*. See how much better that sounds?

Meanwhile, those labeled in common discourse as *Euro-skeptics* or even *anti-Europeans* (excluding the few who genuinely oppose sharing) are in reality *conservatives*. They are people like me who advocate for a *confederal Europe*. The confederal model opposes the centralization of the powers in the EU's central institutions. It does so based on the principle of *subsidiarity* enshrined in the treatises: a collaboration among different institutional levels, where responsibility is assigned to the authority closest to the citizen and the most capable of governing that dimension and that specific material. In practical terms, this means that the most mundane areas closest to citizens' everyday life should remain in the hands of individual member states. This not only protects cultural diversity but also, for example, the unique economic characteristics of each nation. Meanwhile, European institutions should focus on global issues—those dimensions where no individual state can be competitive on its own. Brussels should not attempt to do what Rome can do better, and vice versa.

These are not radical ideas. Many of the founding fathers of Europe believed in the confederal model. It's only today that a sort of ideological single-mindedness has emerged: anyone advocating for a federal Europe is labeled a *friend*, and anyone supporting a confederal Europe is branded an *enemy*. And this doesn't make any sense—not just because we're talking about governance models, where ideology should give way to pragmatic debate—but also because, in practice, the centralizing model promoted by so-called pro-Europeans is proving to be deeply flawed.

In what sense?

Look around you. They told us everything was fine, but when real crises hit—I'm talking about the pandemic and the Russian invasion of Ukraine—we realized just how fragile this construction was. We didn't have a foreign policy strong enough to help prevent the war. We lost control over supply chains—from energy to microchips to active ingredients. We were weak on defense, we didn't have a strategy to defend the continent. Meanwhile, there was no shortage of regulations covering every minor aspect of our everyday lives—from the size of vegetables to how insects should be cooked. I believe that Europe should deal with foreign policy, safe borders, a single market, energy, migration. Individual countries should manage the smaller things, preserving their diversity. There are countless examples, but just to be clear: the needs of a Danish fisherman are very different from those of a fisherman from Mazara del Vallo; the beach resorts on our coastline have a cultural and economic history completely different from that of Normandy; it's hard to manage our immense historical and cultural heritage—even our architectural history—with the same rules used in Finland. And I could go on. In short, I believe that European rules should be less invasive. And it's not a contradiction to say that you can be more Italian, just as you can be more French and more German—and still be European.

So where is it that things didn't work out?

Right from the start. The unification project was not coherent with Europe's history or with the true needs of its peoples. From the creation of the Economic Coal and Steel Community onward, we have expanded our borders and skills in a disorderly and chaotic manner. Today, the Union is a hybrid: we find ourselves dealing with a bureaucratic giant—which we didn't need—without the political giant we desperately do need. And I believe this is also the result of denying its identity from the beginning. Now, the Union has lost any clear sense of its role in history.

Are you referring to the lack of reference to Europe's Judeo-Christian roots in the EU constitution?

Well, that too was a worrying sign—but not because I take a confessional approach. The personal relationship each of us has with God has little to do with it, but it is undeniable that Europe's first borders were drawn by the Benedictine monasteries. And the results are clear to see. I support a secular state—there's no doubt about that. But the Europe that hides crucifixes, bans the use of the word *Christmas* in its official correspondence, and yet allows entire neighborhoods to fall under Islamic law or hosts exhibitions with blasphemous imagery in institutional venues—what exactly is it doing? What I see is a major dichotomy between the historical Europe and today's European Union. Consequently—and unfortunately inevitably—this leads to a growing divide between the sense of being a European citizen and the actual policies of the EU.

True. We could argue about this for hours—perhaps endlessly—but the European Union is the political reality we must come to terms with.

Of course. But this doesn't mean we must always agree and pretend that everything is fine. So, is the person who says we can do better a friend or an enemy of Europe? Because if everything truly were perfect, why did the United Kingdom—a country that joined the European Economic Community in 1973, convinced that its future lay within a free-trade customs area—decide, just a few years ago, to leave the European Union? These are the kinds of questions that we need to ask ourselves—especially if we believe in the value of a strong Europe capable of defending its interests. And since I *do* believe in that vision, I work toward it: to make the Union closer to the interests of its citizens—to restore Europe to the role it once had, and should have again, on the global stage. Before it's too late.

What do you mean by "too late"?

The crises we are facing—and that, unfortunately, we failed to anticipate—could trigger all sorts of reactions. And in my view, if the Union were to fall apart for some reason, whether internal or external to the Union, the real question would not be "What would Italy do?" The real question would be what other nations—those often considered, perhaps naively, to be more pro-European—would do. Nations that, in reality, are very careful about defending their own interests, even at the expense of other member states and of the European Union as a whole.

Who are you referring to? Germany, France, the Netherlands?

I'm just saying that Italy—long seen by some in Brussels as a "difficult" country—is probably one of the firmest, most solid pillars of the European edifice.

Do you think there's an awareness of this in our national debate?

Rarely. Generally, what prevails is a provincial, culturally subordinate approach. European dynamics are far more complex than how they are usually portrayed. It's a mess: there are the member states, there are the national parties, then there's the European Parliament where parties join transnational groups. Then there are the commissioners, the heads of state and the government, all with their own ambitions, needs, and personalities.

How did it feel to enter this context personally?

Paradoxically, I was helped by the surreal narrative the Left had pushed for years—the story of the "monster on its way." When I met the President of the European Council, Charles Michel, for the first time, I joked: "Aren't you surprised to see that I don't have antennas like a Martian?" He was quite amused. But I think that what struck him more was the fact that I wasn't green. Being underestimated—or mischaracterized—can have its advantages in life. I consider myself a serious and rational person, and behaving normally must have come as a positive surprise to many. I believe personal relationships can make a difference: understanding who's sitting across from you helps you find common ground; it allows you to defend your interests while respecting those of others. Knowing foreign languages has been a huge advantage, too. When your thinking isn't mediated—when you can speak freely with others, or speak privately, everything becomes less formal, and much easier. After all, politics is real life, and should be lived as such.

Between you and Macron, judging by appearances, things seem complicated . . .

Appearances can be deceiving. My personal relationship with Emmanuel Macron is a good one. Of course, we don't always agree when it comes to politics. And, let me tell you, from what I've observed, the friction stems more from domestic policies rather than foreign ones.

What do you mean by that?

At first, I couldn't understand the rather aggressive attitude—mostly through the press—coming from some members of the French government.

Especially since, at the same time, France was asking us to intensify our cooperation. Then I realized that the issue had more to do with internal French politics. The French media often draw parallels or simplistic comparisons between me and Marine Le Pen, who is the main opposition figure to Macron's government. In practice, it sometimes feels like I'm being used to settle their domestic disputes. But regardless of who's in power, France cannot ignore the importance of maintaining a solid relationship with Italy.

Are you sure about that?

Let me explain. We need to go back to the complexity of the Union. Two major bodies shape Europe: first, the governments of the member states, and second, European governance. As for the member states, each pursues its own agenda, each one tries to uphold its own national interest based on its own influence—Germany's and France's weight is undeniable, and I respect that—by playing a game of alliances in the European Council. This is the decision-making body that brings together all heads of state, and it can only reach decisions on key issues through broad consensus—or even unanimity. Obviously, such consensus is easier to reach if there is political alignment. Two countries with a socialist government, for instance, will likely have a good base of understanding. But if, on a given issue, their national interests diverge, each will look elsewhere for support. So, we're talking about a constantly shifting game of alliances—one where Italy is a desirable pawn, but also one where Italy must—and can—carry more weight than it has in the past. That's the approach I brought with me the moment I stepped onto the European stage—not the oversimplified narrative I often hear and read about in Italy when people try to describe how European dynamics work.

They say that with you leading the Italian government, the country is isolated in Europe because you've chosen the wrong allies for the European club—like Poland and Hungary.

I've never seen Europe as an exclusive club. That's the vision of those who think there's a first-class and second-class Europe. But Europe isn't a soccer ranking—or at least, it shouldn't be. I respect every nation, with its identities, needs, history, and even their suffering. And that's all the more reason why Eastern European countries—those abandoned to the Soviet yoke after Yalta—deserve respect. Let's debunk a myth: in the European Council, everyone talks to everyone. And that's a good thing. Do you remember the picture of Giuseppe Conte during the long night of Recovery Fund negotiations, chatting amicably with Viktor Orbán to seek his support? The more you can talk to everyone, the more you're able to build solutions. The more you're at the center of the conversation, the better you can defend your country's needs. And there's proof of this. Alessandro—do you know who it was in the European Council who managed to get the minimum taxation on multinationals through? Who overcame the veto votes from Hungary and Poland? When Paolo Gentiloni thanked me for the result, I replied: "This sovereignty politics comes in handy sometimes, don't you think?" That remark was meant to underscore a point: refusing dialogue with certain countries while favoring others doesn't simply the picture, it complicates it.

It's been written that during one of your first appearances at the European Council, you held the floor until the early hours of the morning.

It was the first time we discussed immigration. It was the meeting where we succeeded in including, in the Council's conclusions, the statement that immigration is a European issue—and that protecting its external borders must be a priority. The summit had been scheduled to last two days, but President Michel had suggested working intensively so we could wrap things up by the evening of the first day. By three a.m., we had resolved everything—except one key point concerning NGOs, which, for me, was essential. The others couldn't agree on it. Charles Michel kept trying to persuade me to give up. He kept saying: "Come on, let's end it here." At one point, I turned to him and said: "Charles, this strategy of wearing everyone down is the same one we use in Italy when passing the annual budget law around Christmas. I'm ready to do the same thing here. And I hope everyone else is ready, too, because we're going to be working into the wee hours of the night." Everyone laughed, and we kept working.

The relationship you've developed with some European leaders—judging by the frequent visits to Palazzo Chigi of heads of state and the tone of joint press conferences—was, frankly, unexpected.

Actually, it was unexpected for me, too. Take the Netherlands, for example. As the leader of the so-called "Frugal Countries," it has often been on the opposite side of the European dynamic. And I expect that will happen again. But I found a genuine rapport with the Dutch Prime Minister Mark Rutte, who has since stepped down to become Secretary General of NATO. He's a pragmatic, dynamic person with experience. We talk often and have developed a mutual understanding. Every time the European Council agenda included immigration, we would speak on the phone—and still do. It's a chance to exchange views on what we each hope the conclusions will be. Mark would speak at length. He's interested in curbing secondary movements. I tell him that if they don't help us to stop primary movements, they'll inevitably become secondary ones. There's only one way to align our positions: we must reinforce external border control if we want to protect internal borders. And then I added: "Just imagine how much fun it would be to astonish everyone by entering the Council with a joint position between Italy and the Netherlands on the topic of immigration. Nobody would see it coming." He quickly replied: "Funny, let's work on it." Since then, we've worked well together, even when we don't agree.

But was that the same meeting when you got angry with Macron for not inviting you to the trilateral organized in Paris with Scholz and Zelenskyy, held the day before the Ukrainian president took part in the European Council?

It was the same meeting—but I wasn't angry, as some have claimed, about not being invited. That interpretation is yet another example of the simplistic reading we too often apply to international dynamics—especially in Italy, where we have for too long mistaken foreign policy success for participation in photo ops, even if those photos include people who've just stolen all your jewelry. I don't see things that way. I disagreed with the idea of hosting Zelenskyy on the first day of the Council because the strength of that moment—having the Ukrainian president received by all twenty-seven EU member countries—was diminished by dividing the stage. The invitation has nothing to do with it. And precisely because I think this way, even if I *had* been invited, I wouldn't have gone. If the same meeting had taken place after the Council, I wouldn't have had a problem with it. That time, too, they claimed that by making that statement I had "isolated" myself. That's odd because in Paris, there were only two leaders present, and the other twenty-five hadn't been invited. I said as much—and I doubt I was the only one who felt that way. When it's a question of finding common ground, depending on the measures to be taken, there's always some magic number that must be reached. And to reach that number twenty-seven—unanimity—you need to have everyone's consensus, regardless of any individual country's strength.

Then there's the Commission—that is, the European government. What's your relationship like with Ursula von der Leyen?

Ursula works hard and knows how to listen. It's not difficult to work with her. Of course, holding everything together can't be easy. The European Commission is a constant mediation between the directives of individual nations and the political balance imposed on the European Parliament. The current Commission is backed by a popular alliance—in Italy, we call them Center-Right moderates or Center-Left socialists and liberals. This kind of alliance is reminiscent of Italy's bad experience with broad government alliances. But with an added aggravating factor: the moderates have been timid, allowing the Left free rein over the political agenda to be dominated by the red and green parties. At least, that was the case until a few months ago. This is why we have the duty to change things. As we've seen in Italy, governments backed by such heterogeneous coalitions—held together by interests that are naturally irreconcilable—end up making policies that lack bravery, devoid of vision. And without vision, without politics, the resulting void is then filled with bureaucracy—the infamous Eurobureaucrats.

Some fear that void could also be filled by lobbyists.

Some recent scandals, especially the investigation known as Qatargate, are proof that this danger is very real. I fear that political weakness is leaving Europe vulnerable to influence by private actors and non-European countries whose interests are not always transparent. Qatargate was a wake-up call that put the problem in focus. On the one hand, we need better regulation of how interests are represented—this applies to both private entities and NGOs—and on the other hand, we need to prevent external interferences in the European democratic process.

How do we reverse this trend?

With politics. Until now, the conservatives have kept to the sidelines, but the fact that the EU's third-largest nation (in terms of importance) is now governed by conservatives is significant for the entire Union. If we dismantle the "danger" narrative that the mainstream media has fueled for years to discredit us, we can open up a new path. Among other things, together with my colleagues from Poland and the Czech Republic—who are also members of the political family of the European Conservatives and Reformists group (ECR)—we represent 24 percent of the European population. That's not exactly a small figure. One out of four Europeans lives in a country directly governed by conservatives. And that's not counting those who live under governments that include conservative parties. What we need is a path that will put politics back at the center—to allow distinct visions to exist, to engage in respectful debate. If we prove, as we are doing, that a right-wing government in a major European democracy can be serious, reliable, and consistent; if our long-dismissed policy proposal turns out to be effective, then what happened here in Italy can happen elsewhere. The 2024 European elections could mark the start of a new chapter. Of course, that also means that from now until that electoral deadline, attacks on us may intensify. Clearly, the stakes are very high.

Let's sum things up a bit. Since 2020, you've been the President of the European Conservatives and Reformists (ECR) Party, which currently has sixty-six MEPs in Brussels, elected from the conservative parties in sixteen countries. Aside from Brothers of Italy, these include

Spain's Vox, and Poland's Law and Justice party, led by Prime Minister Mateusz Morawiecki, as well as the Czech Prime Minister Petr Fiala's party, to name a few. In the European Parliament, the ECR is currently in opposition to the Popular Party-Socialist axis that drives much of the EU dynamics. Do you think that model can change? Could a different majority emerge—say, between the Popular parties and the Conservatives, replicating the model of the Center-Right coalition in Italy?

It's too soon to say—both in terms of numbers and political alignments. But I do believe that instead of having majorities that are too heterogeneous, Europe would benefit from a healthy bipolar system. One that allows voters to choose a clear direction at such a decisive moment in our shared European history.

What's your relationship with the European People's Party?

I know Manfred Weber, and I can't deny that after years of limited dialogue, he's shown increasing openness to the concerns we conservatives raise—on sensitive issues for both political families. A case in point is the greater involvement of all European countries in containing and regulating immigration, and of the problems created by certain ideological trends in the ecological transition agenda. What I believe is fundamental here is to talk to each other, to move past preconceptions. That's what I do every day with my fellow prime ministers from the European People's Party (EPP), in a climate of friendship and harmony. I sense a genuine interest in the Italian Center-Right model of governance. But these are long journeys—built on consistent work, not words. In any case, Europe needs to make bold choices. And I believe that can only happen if we put politics back at the center and build a majority based not on identical visions, but at least on homogeneous and compatible ones.

Regardless of election results, though, the France-Germany axis will remain unavoidable.

In parliamentary dynamics, it's not about states. In every country, there's a Right and a Left, conservatives and progressives—call them what you will. You can't "do without" anyone, you need to build alliances around shared ideas that can bring together a range of nations. As the ECR's founding statute states: "respect and equal treatment for all the member states of the Union, old and new, large and small."

You mentioned common defense. Are you in favor of creating a European army—a topic that is, alas, quite relevant now?

Obviously, I support the idea of a Europe that arms itself and has a strong defense system. That said, we have NATO—and we're members of NATO. So, if you're talking about building a European army on top of NATO, then you're creating an overlap—something that's useless, or a poor substitute. The alternative, which we've long advocated for, is to establish a European branch within NATO. Also because . . .

Also because . . . ?

It makes me smile when I hear those who tear their hair out in despair at the US dominating NATO also complain about European countries spending too much on defense. It has to be one or the other. Either we increase our economic contribution to NATO so that we can have a real voice with greater authority and influence—or we accept that the ones defending us will decide for us. This imbalance is a problem, no doubt—especially since, even just for simple geographical reasons, European and American interests don't always align perfectly. So, the best way to strengthen the transatlantic alliance, in my opinion, is to build an equilibrium between the European and American sides. But that comes at a cost in terms of defense investments. Freedom has a cost, it isn't free.

Some accuse you of being beholden to the Americans . . .

Most of the people who say that are experts in sycophancy themselves. As a patriot, I've never been a slave to a foreign power, nor do I seek favor with one country or another, whether near or far. Today, the real enemies of our freedom are those who tell us not to invest in defense—because they want to condemn us to insignificance, and to allow others to decide for us. Or worse because they're still doing the bidding of today's adversaries around the world, just like the fake pacifists who were funded by the Soviet Union. I see things differently. To me, defending the Italian national interest means fully belonging to the Western world—in this context, this means being a serious and credible ally. One that does its part when necessary and earns respect when it stands up for its own interests. That's the Italy I want to represent for as long as I'm Prime Minister.

Giorgia's Agenda

Far from Capalbio

Seneca once said, "The first art that those who aspire to power must learn is that of being able to endure hatred." I read this maxim years ago, and it comes to mind now as I watch Giorgia Meloni seated across from me at her desk. She writes with a green ink pen, her handwriting neat and small, filling the page of a black-bound notebook. I like to imagine it's a kind of secret diary—something to be reread someday, with someone, somewhere, or maybe never, by no one at all. Then again, perhaps that's not the case. More likely, she's mapping out what she needs to do or say tomorrow. Her meticulousness is well known.

It is evening, the close of a day that began with a press conference—hardly an exhilarating one, and full of the usual bias—although things are finally starting to move in the right direction. I'd like to tell her about the Seneca quote, to ask how much she's willing to endure, to inquire about those notes. But I hold back. It would feel like meddling. She seems completely immersed in thought. At last, she closes the notebook, wraps an elastic band around it, and looks up.

"Here I am. I'm ready. Let's get started."

Prime Minister, were you aware that governing would mean dealing with a new problem every day? Some have even said you should be ashamed for singing at Matteo Salvini's fiftieth birthday party.

I'm not at all ashamed. If something made me feel ashamed, I simply wouldn't do it. I was happy to celebrate Matteo's birthday—just as I'm happy about the relationship we have today, which is not just political. I believe that when a team wins an election, finding time to be together outside our institutional roles is a precious thing. Matteo and I do so often, and it's transformed our relationship.

But they say that within the majority, you're always arguing . . .

I don't know what they say—because, as everyone knows, I don't read the newspapers much. Every now and then, ministers or other members of the majority message me to deny what's been written about them in the newspapers. I always reply the same way: don't worry, I have no idea what you're talking about—and I'm not interested in finding out. What matters to me are the facts. And the fact is that, since the dawn of time, you can judge the strength of a majority by how quickly it makes decisions. In just a few months, we've achieved a lot: we passed a budget law in record time, we launched long-delayed reforms—and you can only do that if you're working as a team. What many people don't realize about this government is that most of us came to our posts after a lifetime devoted to politics. Matteo and I, for example, first met when we were young, as leaders of our respective parties' youth movements. Antonio Tajani—another minister I work closely with and have fun while doing so—entered politics when he was twelve. The same is true for Giancarlo Giorgetti. Most members of government have followed a similar path. We're all people who have spent our lives proving that we want to, and are able to, serve our country. For many of us, a failure of this government would be the betrayal of a lifetime. That's something people who haven't walked the same path don't see, especially when they assume that local squabbles could bring down the government.

Still, there seems to be a coordinated attack on you personally.

If we're talking about serious matters, then yes—I was fully aware that I would be taking office during what's arguably the most difficult moment Italy has faced since the end of World War II. If I hadn't been aware of the challenges and responsibilities involved, I'd be completely unfit for the job. I know it won't be easy. Mistakes may happen. Failure is a possibility. But until now, you'll notice, the criticisms and attacks have focused on marginal or opportunistic issues—things that are often irrelevant or even downright stupid. Some are completely fabricated. That should make me angry, but instead I find it reassuring. For two reasons. First: when people have to distort reality to attack you, it means they really don't have anything real to accuse you of. And the public is more attuned to what's real than the newspapers give them credit for. Second: the rage and venom coming from the Left reveals their weakness. They expected this government to be incompetent, ridiculous, and isolated. Instead, they've found one that is serious, results-driven, internationally respected, and unwilling to take orders from them. They've been caught off guard, and they're lashing out. That's a good sign.

Well, no one likes to lose.

That, I can understand. But let's be honest: the issue here isn't that they're angry because their ideas lost. The impression—based on the Left's priorities—is that what really terrifies them is the loss of power that they've held on to for so long, even after they no longer had an identity. They enjoyed a kind of guaranteed access to resources and power, a system that protected them at every level and dispensed social prestige. In other words, it's the only job center they ever got to function properly.

Imagine someone spending thousands of euros to belong to the "right" tennis club. They may not know how to hold a racket, but they're there to meet the right people and to network with those who have connections in the establishment, who can get a deal closed or a job arranged with a single phone call. Now imagine how unhappy those people are who spend thousands of euros a month to rent a villa in Capalbio for the same reason. And suddenly, they realize they're wasting their money—because the people actually making decisions aren't part of that world. You won't find them at those beaches.

Interesting, although perhaps a bit simplistic.

What amazes me is how many of the Left's main battles in recent months have centered not on policy, but on positions of power. From RAI to state-owned companies, from reconstruction agencies to bureaucratic appointments—what seems to concern them most is that we've touched these "branches of power." What's ironic is that, after having occupied every possible seat themselves, they now tear their hair out in despair when we apply a merit-based approach. I have no problem keeping competent people in key roles, even if they're from the Left—and I've proven that. They did not do the same. But they should know that I won't keep someone in a position of responsibility if they're not up to the task, simply because they're protected by someone influential. That's not how I operate. In any case, if the Left wants to base their politics on this, that's fine with me. The Italian people will judge.

At RAI, some say you're carrying out a purge.

Honestly, that's not how I see it. What we're doing is rebalancing—a necessary step, considering the Left still occupies 75 percent of the posts at a state broadcaster funded by *all* Italian citizens. And this rebalancing doesn't just favor the Center Right—it also gives space to other opposition forces who've been crushed under the Democratic Party's excessive dominance. In any case, we didn't throw anyone out. From Fazio to Annunziata, several people chose to leave after the CEO appointed by the previous government resigned, and a new one was brought in. Their reasons seem more linked to new opportunities—or new salaries—than to political pressure. And that deserves reflection. Why would someone leave if no one is pressuring them, just because there's a change in government and leadership? My impression is that some individuals felt protected by the previous system. Now that those safeguards are gone, the environment is more competitive. And perhaps not everyone feels at ease in a system of free competition.

I've heard it said that with Fazio's departure, public television has lost credibility. I respect everyone's opinion, but I have to say, I cringed when

Fazio, while interviewing the French President Macron, remarked: "They say Paris is the capital of Italy." There isn't a single Italian—from the Alps to Pantelleria—who has ever believed anything that absurd. Such a brazen act of servility did not reflect well on our public broadcaster. That said, I very much appreciated Fabio Fazio's professionalism when he stated there had been no purge against him.

The Italian historian and statesman Francesco Guicciardini was already saying this about Italians five hundred years ago: each individual focuses on their own particular situation, on whatever is good for them.

I could never contradict someone who used the informal *tu* to address Machiavelli, and who wrote the masterpiece *The History of Italy.* But I don't believe that Italy is like that. It was a certain system—one that rewarded taking sides over merit—that made people think the best way to succeed was to spend time with the right people, say the right things, and join the right political party. Many Italians found themselves going along with that system just to live in peace. But I'm convinced that if we offer another model—one based on merit, not alliances or favoritism—we can release unbridled energy. And we, first of all, must set an example. That's exactly what we intend to do. We're part of that majority of Italians who don't do and say things just for the sake of opportunism. Those who thrived under the old system will just have to get over it: the party is over.

You're accused of consolidating power.

Of course—because they judge us according to their own way of thinking. In fact, they're already doing it, with no regard for self-awareness or decency. But I'm not afraid. I welcome the comparison—how we operate versus how they operated. I won't be intimidated, especially because this isn't just about nominations. There's a broader, unacceptable narrative that needs to be dismantled.

Which narrative?

The idea that all the good and honest people are on the Left, while all the bad and stupid ones are on the Right. This belief is used to justify all kinds of nastiness and aggression against anyone deemed "dystonic" or out of step with a certain mainstream. It's a narrative that must be challenged because the survival of democracy depends on it. And look, the crazy thing is that those who are always eager to label others as unacceptable are often the first to side with the truly unacceptable.

Can you give me some examples?

Take the case of the anarchist Alfredo Cospito. He was sentenced to ten years and eight months for kneecapping Roberto Adinolfi, the CEO of the Italian nuclear power company Ansaldo Nucleare, and later to twenty-three years for bombing a Carabinieri training barracks. Who imposed the harshest prison conditions on him? Not us. That decision was made in May 2022, when Mario Draghi was Prime Minister, leading a government that included the Democratic Party and the Five Star Movement. The Minister of Justice at the time, Marta Cartabia, made the call based on reports from several independent judicial authorities. Were there any protests back then? No. Then, in October, our government took office—and Cospito began a hunger strike to protest his solitary confinement. Anarchists across half of Europe began attacking Italian officials, blowing up their cars, in an attempt to intimidate the state. And what did some members of the Democratic Party do? They went to visit Cospito in prison and, in essence, suggested that the state should yield to that pressure—calling for the 41-bis regime to be lifted for Cospito. In effect, they tried to portray the poor kneecapper as a martyr, and the right-wing government as the aggressor. Turning the terrorist into a victim, and the victim—that is, the state—into a terrorist. It's a deliberate reversal of the truth for political purposes. And we're not the only ones saying it.

A lot was said, for instance, about the comments made by Valerio De Molli, CEO of Ambrosetti—a globally known management consulting firm famous for organizing the annual Forum Ambrosetti in Cernobbio. On Twitter, he wrote, "Can I say something that no one dares to say because it is not very politically correct: why all these niceties for a bastard killer who is on a hunger strike in prison? He kneecapped a manager and placed two bombs in a training school for carabinieri. May he die on his hunger strike."

That said, we will abide by the decisions made by magistrates, case by case. De Molli's statement is certainly strong, but I'm not surprised by it—especially coming from someone who lives a very international life. Outside of Italy, controversies like this often seem surreal, even absurd, particularly in circles far removed from any reactionary politics, such as those in which De Molli operates. The truth is, we're talking about a man—Cospito—who, in a letter where he boasted about kneecapping Adinolfi, wrote: "On a lovely morning in May I acted, and in those few hours I enjoyed life to the full." Now he's on a hunger strike—a tactic he's used before. On that occasion, he was released from prison by the then–head of state. The message seems to be: if someone kneecaps another person but is on the Left, all they need to do is go on a hunger strike—and the Left will rally to their defense, saying: "Poor Cospito."

In the United States, by contrast, a federal court recently rejected—for the sixteenth time—the request for conditional parole for Sirhan Sirhan, who has spent fifty years in prison for having assassinating Robert Kennedy. He's now nearly eighty years old. And no one—not even the Democrats—was shocked or indignant.

Selective "garantismo"—a belief in procedural guarantees only when it suits political sympathies—is a very Italian concept.

True, and we're right back to square one: the distorted cultural hegemony of the Left, where right and wrong are not measured by codes and laws, but shift according to political convenience.

In what sense?

Here's another example. When I was in the opposition, the Left publicly accused me—explicitly and in this order—of being: morally responsible for the deaths of children who drowned in the Mediterranean Sea; the moral instigator of the murder of poor Willy Monteiro Duarte; and in collusion with all far-right extremist organizations. Then, during a debate at the swearing-in of my regional governor, Five Star Movement Senator Roberto Scarpinato—an influential former magistrate—openly suggested that my party and my government were colluding with terrorists and the Mafia. And yet, no one expressed outrage at those surreal and defamatory accusations.

Fast-forward to when we took office: one of my excellent representatives, Giovanni Donzelli, raised a question in Parliament. He referred to a visit made by four Democratic Party members to the anarchist Alfredo Cospito. During the visit, at Cospito's own request, they spent time talking—and this is the worst part—to some Mafia detainees clearly in cahoots with Cospito to get the 41-bis regime abolished. Donzelli asked this in the chamber: "I want to know whether this Left stands with the state or with terrorists and the Mafia. And we want to know that here, in this House, today."

Good God, all hell was about to break loose.

Exactly. So how do things stand? They can call me a mafiosa, a murderer, a terrorist sympathizer, even a bastard, and no one says anything. But if we raise a pointed question with the Left about an ambiguous yet specific fact, then that's a violation of the Constitution?

In that case, as we know, there was confidential information involved.

But the facts weren't classified, as has been confirmed at various levels. What's amusing is that the details Donzelli referred to were already in the newspapers. That, in fact, was Giovanni's main misstep: if he had said exactly the same thing but cited the press as his source instead of that document, no one would have uttered a word. Because those who were outraged that sensitive facts were mentioned in Parliament said nothing when the same information was published by their friendly newspapers. Once again—it's okay when *they* do it, but others can't.

It's a short step from Donzelli to Undersecretary of Justice Andrea Delmastro. He's the one who told Donzelli about the representatives of the Democratic Party going to see Cospito.

That's right. And for that, he was even subjected to an investigation—for disclosing information protected by professional secrecy. And do you know how we found out? Through the newspapers—they publicized that he was being investigated, in clear violation of the legal requirement for confidentiality in ongoing investigations. Then, the public prosecutor requested that the case be dismissed. But the GIP [Judge for Preliminary Investigations] in Rome ordered a mandatory indictment of Delmastro—a rare move in our justice system—and ordered the case to trial. A decision that seems to be of a political nature.

You're saying the game was rigged.

What I'm saying is that I want a country where rules are respected and applied equally to everyone. A country where those in positions of authority act with loyalty and honor, and don't twist the rules to fit their personal ideology. Look, I'm still shocked about the case of Carola Rackete, the German activist and captain of an NGO migrant rescue vessel. In June 2019, she docked without authorization at the port of Lampedusa and, in doing so, rammed a patrol boat belonging to the Guardia di Finanza.

We all remember that—people still talk about it.

Exactly. And yet, the Left managed to turn this woman into some sort of hero. It was established—also after a court ruling—that broadsiding a vessel of the Italian Military Navy isn't always a crime. I find that deeply troubling because it reflects a dangerous belief that the Left often promotes: that if an action serves their ideology, it's acceptable—even laudable—to break the law of the state. And you can even be rewarded for doing so with a candidacy in the next European elections.

But Matteo Salvini was involved in the incident with Rackete . . .

That's right—and that's exactly why I'm concerned. I'm afraid people won't judge objectively according to the law, but instead based on who holds the office of Minister of the Interior. I was shocked to read an intercepted exchange between two magistrates . . .

The message came from Paolo Auriemma, the Chief Prosecutor of Viterbo, writing to the then-member of the High Council of the Judiciary (CSM), Luca Palamara. Auriemma wrote: "I'm sorry to have to say that I really don't understand where Salvini is wrong. Attacking him now is ridiculous . . . Everyone thinks he did the right thing." To which the influential Palamara replied: "You're right, but now we have no choice but to attack him."

And I remember reading about another troubling wiretap in the case of Mimmo Lucano, the Mayor of Riace, who was convicted for irregularities related to his management of a migrant reception program—an issue very dear to the Left. Despite being sentenced to a first-degree prison sentence of thirteen years and two months, he became a hero in those circles.

Then there's Emilio Sirianni, a Catanzaro judge, widely considered a leading figure in the judiciary associated with the Left. In a phone conversation, he reassured Lucano, who had come under investigation: "Don't worry, these judges are young people who grew up watching Berlusconi's television . . . There's us, judges from the Democratic Magistrature. We're not impartial judges. What I mean is that we are not indifferent—we are biased. We stand with the weak."

Get it? The underlying message is this: *we are above the law.* We are the "good," and in the name of that good, we are entitled to bend the law to our will. Absolutely frightening. But we're working hard to change this Italy we're describing. Because the only way for civilization to defend the weak is to make just laws, applied equally to everyone.

How?

We're not going to do the opposite of what the Left did. If you break the law, if you don't follow the rules, if you fail to do your job, it makes no difference to me whether you're on the Right or the Left. Enough with the hypocrisy of double standards, and enough with the disgrace of those who use public office to pursue their personal or partisan interests. How is it possible that if right-wing students are accused—whether they were the aggressors or the victims will be determined later—of beating up left-wing students in Florence, the entire country stops in outrage, while if left-wing students are investigated—as happened recently in Bologna—for beating and threatening to kill right-wing students, the incident doesn't even make the news? The double standards we've seen in recent years are an evil that we must fight. On this, we're very different from the Left.

But what the Minister of Education and Merit Giuseppe Valditara had to say about the student clashes in Florence was not well received.

Wrong. What wasn't well received was the version of events the left-wing press falsely attributed to Minister Valditara. That's very different—and, above all, it's false. Valditara never threatened the school principal who wrote a letter about the incident, nor did he criticize her for condemning violence. Minister Valditara said something different: that a school principal should not write that any person who believes that national borders matter is automatically a fascist. That is ideological propaganda put forward in a school funded by taxpayers. And you can't do that. Political indoctrination in schools, which the Left has promoted for fifty years, cannot exist in a democratic system. It exists in regimes, where the goal of education is to put ideas in your mind that serve those in power. And let me add: I don't recall any particular cases of conservative teachers abusing their authority to shape students' thinking. But if they ever did, it would be just as unacceptable.

And yet, schools remain a venue for the political battles of the Left.

That's right. Instead of teaching students how to read and write, they think they can teach them how to live—what's right and wrong, who's good and who's bad. And the most incredible thing is that in this context, *we're* the ones labeled intolerant, and *they're* the ones who are tolerant. We're cast as the bad guys; they're the good guys. But the facts tell a different story. We don't discriminate against people just because they're on the Left. They, on the other hand, have always treated those on the Right as pariahs—and discriminated against them. If you look closely, they're the ones taking advantage and being intolerant.

You'll never find young members of Brothers of Italy attacking people handing out leaflets outside a school, or provoking speakers at left-wing assemblies. But during my most recent electoral campaign, this happened to me repeatedly. Groups of left-wing thugs infiltrated my events, trying to provoke fights so they could then claim: "See? The Right is violent." They were hoping that, sooner or later, fists would fly. At one point, I had to reach out to the then–Minister of the Interior and publicly denounce what was happening. And allow me to add: you will never see university students on the Right preventing a minister from presenting a book about his family's history at a book fair—an event that should represent a marketplace for ideas.

Take the case of Eugenia Maria Roccella, Minister for the Family. What struck me most was not what happened to her—which, unfortunately, has become rather common—but the brazenness of the response from Democratic Party Secretary Elly Schlein, who said: "This government has a problem with dissent." If the Secretary of Italy's second-largest party cannot distinguish between dissent and censure, then we have a serious problem. And we truly do—because this is the idea of democracy held by those who are self-proclaimed democrats: a belief that they can engage in behavior that would shock them if done by others. Here's what I mean. Do you know what would have happened if young people on the Right had blocked a Democratic Party minister from speaking—and I had defended them? The incident would have been all over the news, including abroad. There would have been an outcry from reporters, politicians, and commentators. But in this case? No one said a word. They apply double standards to everything, yet still believe they can teach you about morality. I believe many people—even those who once felt aligned with the Left—are concerned about this extremist drift it is undergoing.

You're the ones accused of being extremists.

The Italian and Western Left is increasingly adopting the characteristics of fundamentalist thinking: the unwavering belief that they alone possess the truth, that they are the agents of good fighting against evil. This is the same kind of distorted worldview in which religious Islamic extremism thrives—and it is now mirrored in the Left's growing intolerance. It's a very dangerous phenomenon. Because when you believe you're in the right and your adversary is a cancer on humanity and the planet, then any means of defeating them becomes justified—lies, mud-slinging carried out to perfection by ideologically driven journalists, politically motivated trials, even violence.

How do we fight it?

By restoring the law—the true, constitutionally grounded Rule of Law. A system where the rules apply equally to everyone, without distinctions between first- and second-class citizens based on what party they vote for. In Italy, until now, it hasn't been this way. I am working so that it will be. Because if the rules are equal, then rights are equal, too—starting with the right to govern if the Italian people decide that's what they want you to do. And that right should not be undermined by those who try to sabotage your efforts—not because you're failing at your job, but because you're not doing what *they* want you to do.

Italy, Land of the Unassured

How to Defuse the Social Bomb

It can happen that, in the middle of a conversation, one has to stop. This time, it's because of a phone call from the head of state: "Excuse me, Giorgia, but President Mattarella is on the line," an assistant informs her. I leave the room and take the opportunity to drink yet another coffee—one more for the day, which is now coming to an end. About ten minutes go by, and I step back into her office. I ask, "Any problems?" "Here, problems are the norm," she says, clearly dealing with yet another issue. A brief pause, then she adds, "In this job, the most accurate prediction you can make is that something unexpected will happen. The biggest problem is that the constant state of emergency makes it impossible to plan your time. For me, someone who is used to organizing everything, that's a real issue. Also because you're forced to put yourself—and, tragically, your family—at the bottom of the list. Not that I was a stay-at-home mom before, let's be clear. I've always been a mother who isn't around enough, but this way, it's really tough. Fortunately, Andrea and Ginevra are used to it, and we're a well-trained, united, and supportive team." I feel slightly guilty for being the reason more precious minutes of her private life are taken away, but there's very little time left to finish this story—so we continue.

Let's talk about welfare, the set of benefits and services, whether monetary or not, delivered in favor of people with the aim of improving the quality of life and the well-being of workers and their families. In Italy, depending on how it's calculated, it's worth between 27 percent and 30 percent of the GDP.

A very important figure that ranks at the top for expenditure on social services. But allow me to make a necessary premise.

Please do.

The principle we must start from—one that should be obvious but, in Italy, doesn't seem to be—is that wealth is not created by the state. Wealth is created by businesses and workers. What the state can and must do is redistribute the share that pertains to it. Its goal should be to put these people—entrepreneurs as well as workers—in the best possible conditions to generate as much wealth as possible. So far, however, the messages sent out on this issue have been very misleading.

Such as?

Things like the idea that the state creates jobs and can therefore guarantee them by decree—just as it can abolish poverty by decree—and other such absurdities. Unfortunately, that's not the way it goes. Outside of the failed system of real socialism, the state does not create jobs. What the state does is set the rules within which the labor market operates—it can certainly encourage it or, alternatively, hinder it. Its role, then, is to devise the most effective regulations so that citizens can create wealth through work. The virtuous cycle is: more jobs, more wealth, more tax revenues, and thus more resources for the state to support those who lag behind—helping to buffer social inequalities. The alternative has already been seen in Communist regimes: the "equal distribution of misery."

That's why you're against universal income in the way in which it was conceived by the Conte government?

I remember the evening of the announcement: "We have abolished poverty," said the then-Deputy Prime Minister Luigi Di Maio from the balcony of this very same building overlooking Piazza Colonna, popping open a bottle of sparkling wine. At the time, I thought, this show will come back to haunt the Five Star Movement. And I wasn't wrong. Because at the core of that celebration was a massive lie. And the lie wasn't just that the Reddito di Cittadinanza [universal basic income, or citizens' income] was the wrong tool to eliminate poverty—it was the very idea that poverty could be abolished via government decree. Years later, the Five Star Movement came up with another lie: that with the 110 percent Superbonus [*a tax incentive that provides a 110 percent deduction on the cost of certain renovations, primarily focused on energy efficiency and seismic safety improvements for residential buildings—Translator's Note*], you could make your home energy-efficient for free. When critics pointed out that this so-called free program had cost the state tens of billions, Giuseppe Conte responded by saying he had never claimed the Superbonus was free for the state, only for the citizens. I was stunned. Do these people really not understand that the money the state spends belongs to all of us? If the government spends money in one place, it has to take it from somewhere else. The Superbonus ended up costing around €2,000 per person for every Italian—including those who never used it and even those who don't own a home. And all this to improve the energy efficiency of less than 4 percent of Italy's real estate—mostly second or third homes, including six castles. In short, an enormous use of resources that primarily benefited those who were already well-off. And on top of that, there was the lie about credit transfers—a clumsy and thinly veiled attempt to create a state currency to avoid paying interest to financial markets. But in the end, banks charged up to 30 percent in fees to cash in on these credits. A great deal for the banks. . . . The measure never actually guaranteed that people could sell their credits—only that they had the option to do so. But soon, businesses, banks, and financial operators found themselves overloaded with these credits and stopped accepting them. As a result, thousands of companies and families were left in great financial difficulty. This is the situation the current government inherited from the charlatans of "everything for free"—and one it is now trying to fix. That said, going back to universal income, beyond everything we've already discussed, there's an even more fundamental cultural issue at play.

Which one?

It's a terrible mistake to equate those who can work with those who cannot. Doing so ultimately discriminates against the most vulnerable—those who are genuinely unable to work. Consider this paradox: with universal income, a perfectly healthy twenty-year-old could receive up to €780 per month, the same maximum amount granted to a person with a disability. Is that a fair system? And, moreover, is it fair for the young person who is capable of working? I don't think so. Because the message the state was sending to that young person was, above all, that they weren't needed. A message that was both simple and shocking: "Stay home because you're of no use to me. And if you're struggling, I'm not interested in helping you improve your situation—I can't save you." Setting aside the humiliation—can a country really afford to do without anyone who is of working age and in good health? I don't think so. I believe we definitely need everyone's contribution, and that we must encourage everyone to improve their personal situation—because by doing so, they also improve the nation as a whole. I believe that work—any kind of work—brings with it a sense of value and dignity that sitting at home doing nothing will never provide. I find it deeply wrong to tell someone that it's better not to work at all than to accept a job that doesn't perfectly align with their education or aspirations. Because every job teaches you something and helps you grow. And any door can open a thousand others—while the door to your home is unlikely to be knocked on by someone offering you your dream job. Nothing happens unless you are willing, first and foremost, to throw yourself into the fray, to challenge yourself. I've been through it myself—that's why I know this to be true.

Doing what?

Today, I am the Prime Minister, but I started out cleaning houses. And I did many other jobs that some people today might consider unsuitable—maybe even humiliating. I worked as a babysitter, a waitress, a cloakroom attendant, a barista, at the Porta Portese market, and as an English tutor. I did whatever it took to support myself honestly. And let me tell you—those jobs taught me a lot. That's how I learned to respect work in all its forms. I left school with very high grades, but I never thought that that meant I should sit on the couch waiting for the perfect opportunity to just come along. And besides, I had no other choice—because, fortunately, the universal income law didn't exist yet.

What do you mean when you say you didn't have a choice?

I didn't grow up in a wealthy family. My mother went to great lengths to support me until I finished high school. But as soon as I got my diploma, she expected me to contribute to the family's expenses—just as my sister, Arianna, had already been doing for years. As the older sister, Arianna had to leave school to help support our family and allow me to continue my studies. That's why she didn't get her diploma until many years later as a private student. Try explaining that to those journalists who can't stand the idea that someone might have succeeded from nothing rather than by having the right connections. Now, they're trying to distort reality—painting my mother as a real estate speculator and my family as well off. What do they know? Anyway, let's get back to the point: out of all of us, I was the most protected, the one most shielded from hardships. So, it was only right that the day after I left school, I started pulling my weight. My mother told me that from that moment on, I would have to contribute to the household expenses—and that's exactly what I did.

So what did you do?

I started looking for work and accepted whatever I could find. I couldn't afford to wait for something I liked. But I was also involved in politics, which was my passion, so I preferred odd jobs—working in the evenings, mornings, or on Sundays—to keep some afternoons free for campaigning. At one point, I found myself juggling five jobs at the same time, just to make the one million lire I brought home each month, plus a little extra for myself—so that I could live my life. But honestly, I tell this story with pride, and I will never stop thanking my mother for making me stand on my own two feet. That was one of the greatest lessons of my life—far more valuable than any government handout. That's why I find it so frustrating when I hear people say they accept universal income because they prefer it over a job they consider below their expectations.

Do these people ever stop to think where that money comes from? It's paid for by taxes—taxes from all those people who took jobs that weren't in line with their own expectations. Isn't that a huge injustice? That said, of course, our goal is to create the conditions for everyone to find a job that matches their skills and qualifications as closely as possible.

You're talking to an ex-porter, a gas pump attendant, a deckhand. Insofar as you—but not I—are young, let's talk about other times and other families.

I can't imagine you dressed as a deckhand [*laughs*]. Look, on the subject of family, I completely agree. I often wonder if I will ever be as strict with Ginevra as my mother was with me. To be honest, I don't think so. And here timing comes into play. My mother had me and Arianna when she was barely in her twenties, while I had Ginevra when I was almost forty. I think that having children later tends to make you experience parenthood in a much more apprehensive and protective way, and that isn't necessarily a good thing. Then, again on the topic of timing, I believe that certain principles should be eternal and not change from one generation to the next—even though in practice they often do not. The big difference between the world in which your parents lived and the one in which we live as parents is the crisis of the concept of authority at every level. Unfortunately, we're still riding the long wave of 1968, and that has a significant impact on education. In our grandparents' time, if you misbehaved at school and the teacher told your parents, you'd get a beating. Now, if the same thing happens and the teacher tells your parents, he risks getting the beating instead. If, in fact, your father had sent you as a boy to work as a gas pump attendant, today he might risk arrest—or, at the very least, general disapproval.

But my father today would have the universal income alternative.

Of course, if he met the requirements, he would receive it today. Let's go beyond the propaganda and look at things as they really are. If you're unable to work, have children who are minors to support, or are over sixty years old, you continue to receive universal income. But continuing to give it to a young person who can work means stealing their time. Let's think about this together. Imagine a twenty-year-old guy without a job. Instead of helping him find one, you give him the income subsidy. Okay. For how long can you keep paying him? Given that very few people who received universal income actually found work in the meantime—three years, four years? Sooner or later, you have to take it away from him, because not even the Five Star Movement ever meant that it should become a lifetime entitlement. Now, when you take away his income subsidy after four years—he's now twenty-four—is he richer or poorer than before? He's poorer because he's back to square one, except now he's lost four years. And if, instead, during those four years he had jumped into the job market in some way—even by accepting a job that didn't perfectly match his expectations—would he be richer or poorer? He'd be richer because he'd have more experience, he would have learned a trade, he might have put some money aside, and who knows what doors might have opened for him in the meantime. In short, he would actually be in the job market.

Easier said than done; maybe some people really can't find a job.

I understand your objection. That's why we want to strengthen training opportunities for those looking for work but are unable to find it—because even the time spent learning makes you richer than being supported by the state for a few years. But going back to work, maybe there's a lot more of it available than it seems. Let me put it this way—I'm reminded of that classic scene from many movies, American and otherwise, where a stranger walks into a bar and asks the bartender, "I'm looking for a job." To which the owner replies, "If your papers are in order, you can go in the back and wash dishes." And just like that, the guy earns his day's wage. Of course, that's an oversimplification—no one expects work in Italy to function that way. But at the same time, we can't keep living in the exact opposite reality, where both employers and job seekers struggle to connect legally. The right to work must also mean the right to employability—a state that helps legal job-matching in all its forms instead of hindering it, which only fuels undocumented work and low employment rates. And that's exactly what happened in Italy: We have one of the lowest employment rates in Europe. At the same time, we have one of the highest rates of undocumented work. It almost seems like a paradox for a country that once had the strongest Communist Party in the Western world—but in reality, it's probably the natural consequence of that very history. In the Marxist model of labor and the economy, only large companies exist—whether public or private doesn't really matter. These companies provide traditional jobs to masses of salaried workers. Those who were raised on that vision of society believe that the only legitimate form of employment is a permanent, full-time contract. And never mind the fact that reality tells us otherwise. Rather than face how things actually work, they prefer to cling to their ideological models, ignoring the real labor market. That's how we've gradually witnessed a massive deception: A protected, heavily unionized system that only benefits a portion of salaried workers, presented as if it were the normal state of the job market—while hiding a much broader reality that includes: self-employment, small businesses, nontraditional work agreements, cooperative work, jobs in small enterprises. All of which come with far fewer protections. Italy's top priority must be getting excluded workers into the labor market and expanding protections to all workers, regardless of the type of job they do. This does not mean promoting job insecurity, but it does mean stopping the self-deception that has been going on for far too long.

During one of the meetings at Palazzo Chigi with the trade unions, CGIL Secretary Maurizio Landini very heatedly raised his voice and said: "We need to put an end to this job precariousness!" UIL Secretary Pierpaolo Bombardieri arrived at the table accompanied by a worker who had been temporarily employed for ten years to challenge the government's policies. It was quite easy to politely point out that if job insecurity has continuously increased in Italy and wages have decreased, the blame certainly can't be placed on those who have just taken office. Instead, perhaps, the real responsibility lies with those who have promoted the wrong labor market policies for years. "Well, we actually agree with the unions—things have been managed really poorly up to now. It's time to turn the page," I replied. Stunned expressions around the table.

And besides that, the best part is that since this government took office, employment has been steadily increasing, particularly stable employment and female employment. Under our leadership, Italy has reached its all-time record for the number of permanent jobs. I believe this result is due not only to the measures implemented by the government, such as the reduction of the tax wedge and incentives for hiring, but also to a renewed sense of trust among businesses and workers toward the state. Yes, the message we have sent is clear: we stand with those who want to work hard, start businesses, take initiative, become self-employed, and make the most of their skills, education, and determination in a salaried job. And that message has been received. We are proud of this, and we absolutely intend to continue down this path.

They will accuse you of wanting to cut worker safeguards.

It's quite the opposite. What we want to do is not reduce worker protections, but rather make them universal. We want to burst the bubble that allows a few to live in a protected world while many—far too many—are left without any protections at all. The level of worker safeguards should be as high as possible, but it must be equal for all workers. It's not fair to have a system where unionized workers are treated as first-class employees, while those who aren't end up as second-class workers. A worker is a worker, regardless of their contract type or job role. In other words, we don't want to give everyone a universal basic income—we want to give everyone full citizenship in the job market. Because when the job market works, income follows. And when income is earned rather than doled out, it has an entirely different value.

All very logical, but what's your recipe?

There's a lot of work to be done. We started by reducing labor costs—at least for 2023—by cutting payroll taxes by six percentage points for incomes up to €35,000, and by seven points for incomes up to €25,000. This means putting more than €100 extra per month into workers' pockets. Then, we introduced incentives, especially for those hiring with stable contracts, and established rules that allow everyone to work in the way and time frame they prefer without having to do so illegally.

Another key priority is creating a strong connection between labor supply and demand. While we have hundreds of thousands of unemployed people, entire sectors are struggling to find workers—even for well-paid jobs. This is particularly true in industries linked to Made in Italy, one of our country's most valuable assets. For this reason, we created the Made in Italy High School—because at the root of it all, we need a cultural revolution that moves forward on multiple fronts.

Let's hear what they are.

The first principle, as we mentioned before, is merit—and not just in education. The disaster of 1968, with everyone being given the same passing grade in the exams they took, and a world where equality was imposed at the finish line—resulting in a downward leveling—has caused immeasurable damage to this country. Merit was treated as the enemy of equality, and the result was that people advanced not based on their skills or worth, but through connections and recommendations, regardless of their actual abilities. But equality and merit are not enemies—rather, one is the prerequisite for the other. Equality must be guaranteed at the starting point, and merit must determine the outcome. In other words: I guarantee you a society where your future is not determined by the family or the city you are born into. But where do you end up? Well, that depends on you.

It depends on what you're worth, on what you demonstrate, on what you're willing to sacrifice. This is also the only serious way to stop the so-called "brain drain"—that is, the exodus of capable and deserving people who know they cannot access, or do not want to access, a social elevator based on connections, but are aware that they can prove their talent through facts and actions. A talent that, in Italy, is likely to be hard to recognize.

The Italy of the "recommended" candidates . . .

I came across a statistic published by ISTAT (Italian National Institute of Statistics) that made me think: turning to relatives, friends, and acquaintances remains by far the most common practice for finding a job. The informal channel, personal connections, or word of mouth, always prevails over formal methods, such as sending a résumé or going through a selection process. And as a politician, I'll add that it has always angered me to see people complain about nepotism, but then, when it comes down to it, they're the ones recommending or getting recommended. We need the courage to break this mold or at least get closer to how things work in the English-speaking world.

And how does it work?

It works in such a way that recommendations are made openly and not under the table, but you take responsibility for the person you're recommending. In other words, if the person turns out to be incompetent, your credibility is at stake, too. This is how recommendations are made by professors, for example, through formal letters of recommendation that they sign. And when your name is on the line, you're not recommending a friend's child, but the student who truly deserves it. This means breaking the mold where the leadership class is formed in private clubs, according to closed-shop elites, often made up of incompetent people who just happen to be in the right place at the right time.

Are you saying you're against the elites?

Clearly, every system needs a ruling class; the problem is how one becomes a part of it and how one behaves once they are in. Beyond that, the issue with this perverse system—where merit is treated as an enemy and being part of the right circle is considered a virtue—goes even further: we live in a society where, paradoxically, wealth earned through skill and sacrifice is seen as a problem, while inherited wealth, acquired without effort, is regarded as a value. It's crazy. If you're the heir of a family that has been granted extremely generous highway concessions, allowing you to make a fortune off a public asset without even worrying about infrastructure safety and maintenance, you're welcomed with open arms. If you're a De Benedetti, you pay taxes in Switzerland, run companies that have received millions in bank loans—many of which turned into bad debts that the state later had to bail out with taxpayers' money—you're given a platform to preach on television. But if you're an entrepreneur who built something significant from nothing without asking anyone for anything, and you buy yourself a nice car, you become the target of social envy, and the state looks at you with suspicion. It's the opposite of how it should be. Personal success achieved through merit is a good thing, and wealth created through skill and entrepreneurship benefits society as a whole. And yet, both are often viewed with distrust. Meanwhile, those who owe their position merely to unearned yield or to being part of the right networks are frequently praised in talk shows and the mainstream media.

De Benedetti has said you're an idiot.

We'll talk about that in court, but let it be clear that I consider every single insult from Carlo De Benedetti a badge of honor to wear proudly on my chest. Few things make me as proud of what I have done as being seen as an enemy by characters like him.

Let's move on.

The point is that today there's widespread social envy and a deep-seated aversion to the productive world, something that has to be eliminated.

And who might the envious be?

It's the general climate. We're still living under the dominant post-Communist culture, where the "boss" is automatically seen as a bastard to be fought against, and wealth creation is inevitably associated with dishonesty. Now, dishonest entrepreneurs should, of course, be subject to civil and criminal laws just like any other citizen who breaks the law. But beyond that, it is no longer acceptable for those who start a business to be automatically considered enemies of the state. It's not like the state, as it should and as happens in other countries, says: "Well done, thank you for opening a business and providing jobs. Tell me what you need—how can I help you in some way, since what you're doing benefits me too?" No. Instead, from the very next day, the state starts persecuting them: taxes come raining down, often useless or absurd bureaucratic requirements, and suffocating inspections upon inspections. And those without strong backing eventually give up, thinking: "Why am I even bothering to battle against the windmills?" We need to change direction.

Basically, you're saying that Italy is the enemy of entrepreneurs . . .

I believe that we're stuck in a mental framework, typical of the Left, that no longer exists. They always view the labor market through the same outdated lens: on one side, the employer, who is always the villain, and on the other, the worker, who is always the victim. And in between, there's a whole world of so-called privileged individuals—die-hard tax evaders, according to them—such as the self-employed, freelancers, and all nonunionized workers. But today, the world is much more complex than that. Employers and employees are now both exposed to the same challenges, and they need to move forward together. That's why I firmly believe in forms of worker participation in businesses. I have never met an employer who didn't care about their employees or who didn't understand that getting the best out of them requires ensuring they feel connected to the company and fulfilled in their work. The backbone of Italy's productive sector consists of small entrepreneurs, artisans, and shopkeepers who make sacrifices for the good of their businesses—just as most workers do. Yet, the union-backed Left only sees the latter and considers the former as enemies. This is especially evident when it comes down to labor safeguards.

In what sense?

In the sense that in the current labor market a bubble has formed inside which there are few people with safeguards and "all the world is outside," to put it in the words of one of Italy's most popular singers, Vasco Rossi. But the trade unions don't talk about these millions of workers without safeguards.

Who's inside and who's outside?

Inside the system, there are executives and public- and private-sector employees with fixed schedules and guaranteed salaries, sick leave, paid vacations, pension contributions, and severance pay. Outside, there's a wilderness of the unprotected—freelancers, the employees of micro-businesses, and even workers in cooperatives or undocumented jobs, the precarious, temporary workforce. Focusing only on what happens within this protected bubble means increasing social inequalities.

Look, the brilliant idea of a four-day workweek recently emerged. Sure, it's an intriguing concept, and a large company might theoretically try to implement it. But what about everyone else? Can you imagine a contractor leaving a job unfinished? Have you ever seen a freelancer willingly give up an invoice? Have you ever spoken to a self-employed worker who works sporadically, maybe adjusting their schedule around their spouse's shifts? It really shows the kind of world the people making these proposals think they live in.

But it's not like everything runs smoothly inside the bubble either. If a newly graduated engineer or doctor—after six or more years of studying at universities that are often world-class—earns about the same in their first job as a newly hired waiter, excluding tips, then something is clearly wrong. Don't you think?

The issue of wages—and, consequently, pensions—is one of the pillars of a civilized society, and we certainly have a problem in this regard. But this problem as well is the result of a system that has focused more on protecting those already inside the fortress of job security rather than extending those protections to others. Just think about this paradox: the current ruling class of the country—let's say those in their sixties and older—is probably the only generation that has had more than their parents and more than what their children have or will have, both in terms of opportunities and income, as well as welfare benefits. Those who have governed until now have always pretended this problem didn't exist—after all, young people were young and didn't understand. But now, those young people have grown up—as we mentioned at the beginning of this conversation—and they have become aware that they've been betrayed. Do we still have time to make amends?

It's up to you to tell us.

I believe we do, as long as we think in terms of years rather than months—which is the time frame I envision for the government coalition I lead. We can certainly facilitate, and have already begun to facilitate, renewal processes. We can fight certain outdated privileges, and we can, as we have already done, trigger a gradual reduction of labor taxation.

We can support growth by trusting and encouraging those who create wealth and jobs—something that is also a prerequisite for wage growth. Because the issue of inadequate wages cannot simply be solved by decree, as those who propose a legally mandated minimum wage seem to think, without considering the potential side effects.

They accuse you of being against the increase in the minimum wage.

Do you really think it's possible that someone who, in just a few months, cut payroll taxes to put more money in the paychecks of low-income workers is against raising minimum wages? Do you know what I'm against? I'm against making a mess that backfires on workers and worsens public finances just to score political points. We can't pretend not to understand that in a country with a high percentage of union-negotiated contracts, the minimum wage proposal from the opposition risks becoming not an additional protection, but a replacement—one that could actually drive wages down for many workers. That would be a gift to big economic powers, which the Left, whether they know it or not, has become a mouthpiece for. And besides, if the minimum wage was really the solution, why didn't the Left implement it during the ten years they were in power? In any case, as I've shown, by calling the opposition to the table, that I'm always open and willing to discuss wages—as long as the solutions actually improve things.

And what's needed?

Redistributing safeguards throughout the entire working life. There's another paradox in our system: today, the lower your salary and job position, the fewer safeguards you have. As you progress, the more your responsibilities and salary grow, the more safeguards you receive. So, a researcher can lose their job at any moment, while a full professor becomes untouchable—even if they don't show up for class. In short: the less you earn, the less you matter, and the fewer safeguards you have; the more you earn, the more responsibility you hold, and the more safeguards you receive. In my view, it should be the opposite: the higher the position (and the salary), the easier it should be to remove someone who isn't performing well. It is the ruling class that should always be put to the test and, by definition, be in a precarious position—not ordinary workers. And positions should be earned through merit and value, not simply based on seniority.

But seniority is experience, it's value.

I don't doubt that, of course. What I'm saying is that it shouldn't be an automatic process, as it is in almost all sectors of public employment, though I fear it's no different in the private sector. I believe that salary should always be tied to a productivity assessment, and the greater the responsibility, the more meticulous the assessment should be. Because otherwise, and this is what happens today, when you still have to pay a high salary to someone who isn't as productive as they should be, it's obvious that I can't afford to pay a good salary to a young person who's taking it easy. In my mind, it's the weakest who should be the most protected.

A little earlier you mentioned salaries and pensions. We've already talked about the former, what's your position on the latter?

I think that we don't think enough about the pension problems of the future retirees. We need to be very truthful and sincere about this subject, which I realize will not foster consensus: we need to have the courage to say that the system can't hold the way it does not.

Let's say what this truth is.

I won't back out. Today we have people who retire on average at sixty, and at sixty-seven, at the latest, mainly with the wages-linked system and a pension equal to about 80 percent of the income they received over the last ten years. But tomorrow, with the purely contributory system, people will retire on average at seventy with a pension that will reach 40 percent of their average income, if they're lucky. Over the years, we've pretended not to see that a social bomb is waiting to go off: millions of elderly people will be without a dignified pension income.

Objection. Let's talk about acquired rights.

The point is not to take away rights that have already been acquired but to add rights for those who have few today due to a system that has neglected the younger generations. Let me also say that behind this principle of acquired rights, there are also significant privileges. Think about the so-called "golden pensions"—those who consider a pension of tens of thousands of euros per month an acquired right, even though it is not at all linked to the contributions they paid but rather the result of unfair laws. This happens in the same Italy where someone who has worked their entire life will receive a miserly pension. The cornerstone of the law is that all citizens are equal before the law. When such enormous disparities exist, perhaps you should start asking some questions.

There are some who suggest resolving the question upstream, setting a ceiling for pensions in the Constitution.

This is how it is in Germany—a country where a person can stop working at the age of sixty-seven: there's a maximum limit on the pension paid by the state, regardless of how much you may or may not have contributed. In fact, it's very common for those who can afford it to turn to supplementary pension schemes. After all, a cap on public benefits would not be new for Italy; for salaries, a limit of €240,000 has already been in place for some time.

What can I say, for once we pretend we're Germans?

I would rather focus on being Italians. The main challenge is to generate more wealth by not obstructing the productive sectors. The conservatives' motto is: "Don't disturb those who want to work." The government must inspire optimism, free up energy, and restore trust in institutions and the state—but in a state that doesn't cheat you, that doesn't change the rules every two minutes, that doesn't drown you in bureaucracy or overwhelm you with paperwork, that doesn't take away most of what you earn, that ensures justice without endless delays, and all the other things we know too well. At the same time, it must tackle waste, privilege, and injustice—because we live in a reality where, as we have already said, a small group enjoys excessive protection and guarantees, while many others are left to fend for themselves.

Does the decision to tax banks' windfall or excess profits fall within this rationale?

First, I want to say this: I have the utmost respect for our banking system, which is solid and must be protected. The government has no intention of targeting banks. However, we had to step in to address an imbalance. The European Central Bank's questionable decision to fight inflation through a significant and prolonged increase in interest rates has led to a rise in the cost of money, penalizing families and businesses. On top of this, the banking system has not acted entirely fairly—it was very quick to raise interest rates on mortgages and loans but left the rates offered to savers practically unchanged. This created a distortion that needs to be addressed.

The banks didn't welcome this, and some have spoken of a Socialist regime measure.

Of course, no one likes a tax increase, but I have to say that the criticism has come more from newspapers than from the banks themselves, which have actually reacted very calmly. Those who talk about a Socialist regime have a strange idea of the free market. In a fully competitive environment, windfall profits don't happen so easily. There's a big difference between rent-seeking positions and profits generated by entrepreneurial dynamism. The government intervened on earnings derived from the banks' dominant position, as is necessary to protect a truly free market system. And besides, I don't recall Italian Socialists ever taxing banks—I only remember public money being handed out to them by the Left. This confirms that what we did was a right-wing move—addressing an unfair margin that banks have benefited from in recent months.

It's that word "unfair" that you've repeated several times, I don't think by chance, that has certainly made people prick up their ears.

And I stand by it. You see, the issue is that banks have increased interest rates on lending but not interest rates for savings, the ones they pay to those who deposit their money. This created an economic, not just moral, imbalance, which is why we intervened by introducing a 40 percent tax on the difference between these two rates. Of course, we have put in place all the necessary limits and safeguards to ensure that banks are not put in a difficult situation.

Giuseppe Conte's words were: better late than never.

Yes, indeed: better late than never that the Right has come to power.

Nature with Man Inside

Notes for an Eco-Sustainable Conservatism

In her office, Giorgia Meloni twirls one of her many colorful gel pens in her hand. She's unusually relaxed—perhaps because the latest economic figures are positive, or maybe because evening has fallen, and the day has ended relatively peacefully, a rarity in her world. No media storms triggered by a controversial statement deemed "politically incorrect" by someone in the majority or the government.

"Today," she says, "I'm going to ask *you* a question: Do you know the difference between an environmentalist on the Right and one on the Left?"

Not exactly.

Perfect. Don't feel guilty—you're not alone. I'll tell you what the difference is. The environmentalist on the Left—both in Italy and around the world, as we've learned from observing America—is typically someone who lives in the heart of a big city, often in a traffic-restricted zone, surrounded by comforts and services that consume enormous amounts of energy that produce pollution. This same person, generally speaking, loads up their spacious, powerful SUV on the weekend with a €3,000 mountain bike—obviously equipped with batteries, just in case they get tired—and heads off to cycle along trails in untouched natural areas. It's very trendy these days. Well, the environmentalist on the Right, on the other hand, is the person who *lives* in those untouched areas and works from dawn to dusk to keep them that way, despite the polluting weekend intrusion of the left-wing environmentalist.

Rather paradoxical—but still an effective metaphor.

That's the reality across much of the West. I mentioned America just now: think of the New Yorker who becomes an environmentalist after work in the evenings by attending exhibitions or trendy events, yet scorns the Texan who lives on horseback, lasso in hand, surrounded by cattle. And everyone—I mean, intellectuals and journalists like you—praises the former as erudite and refined, all while snubbing the latter because he works with his hands and doesn't smell like fresh laundry at the end of the day. Or maybe the real reason is that the former is a Democrat, and the latter is a Republican.

Now, I use this paradox to illustrate the very simple distinction between *ideological environmentalism* and *conservative environmentalism*. The former believes that protecting nature requires removing humans from it. The latter believes that nature is protected precisely because humans live in it. Hence, the first rule for saving the environment is to live inside it—to care for it 24/7, 365 days a year. But that's easier said than done. So, caring about the environment means first and foremost caring for the men and women who, with great sacrifice, have chosen to remain in it—like sentinels of civilization—resisting depopulation and abandonment.

We will not save a single plant or wild animal if we fail to protect—both economically and socially—the farmers, breeders, shepherds, residents of rural hamlets, and small business owners who keep the rural and tourist economy alive. In other words, they are the true defenders of the environment, and a conservative government has the duty to stand with them. Roger Scruton put it better than I ever could: "Environmentalism is the quintessential conservative cause, the most vivid instance in the world as we know it of that partnership between the dead, the living, and the unborn."

It is one of your most famous and oft-repeated slogans: "We are for nature with man inside."

And, like all things taken for granted, it sounds almost revolutionary. But I'm not surprised. Another theme I've often spoken on is this: "In times like these, the only way to rebel is to be conservative—that is, preserve what we are." So, since we *are* our planet, it would be unthinkable for a conservative not to make every effort to leave the earth to their children, at least as they received it.

Do you really believe that's possible?

Of course—but not through utopian, surreal, or at times even absurd ideas. The only viable path is for environmental sustainability to progress hand in hand with economic and, consequentially, social sustainability. We must find a balance because humans and nature are not adversaries—they are one and the same. If the planet is unwell, then so is humanity. Nature exists both in the environment and in man. For those who have faith, what Benedict XVI teaches still holds true: "Creation is a gift that has not been given to us to be destroyed, but to become God's garden."

Don't you see the risk of a clash between two forms of catastrophism? In the battle between humans and the environment, will only one prevail?

Not at all. There's no need for such a clash. In fact, I only see one kind of catastrophism. Take Greta Thunberg, for instance. In 2018, she posted on Twitter that the world would end in 2023. The post has since been deleted, but millions of people—young and old—believed her. And I'm sure they did in absolute, genuine good faith. But now that we've reached 2023, maybe her forecast was somewhat ambitious?

I agree that it was daring, and perhaps even premature. But let's return to reality. On the topic of energy transition, the European Union is putting a lot of pressure on its member states.

I assume you know what the original nucleus of the EU was called: the European Coal and Steel Community (ECSC).

The European Coal and Steel Community, established by the Treaty of Paris, signed on April 18, 1951.

That's right, I see you came prepared. What happened was that three men—not just any three men but the French Minister of Foreign Affairs

Robert Schuman, the German Chancellor Konrad Adenauer, and the Italian Prime Minister Alcide De Gasperi—realized something fundamental: Europe had to organize itself to be self-sufficient in energy—then primarily coal—and in the raw materials essential for development, chiefly steel at the time. Together with Belgium, the Netherlands, and Luxembourg, they created a plan to manage those vital resources. What else can we call what they achieved in that spring seventy-two years ago if not a "salvific vision"—the farsighted leadership of three great statesmen whose names still appear in our history books today?

Today, coal is seen as the devil, and steel isn't faring much better since producing it is considered too polluting for the environment.

Naturally, many years have passed since then, and fortunately the world has moved forward. But, as we've already said: without a vision, there are no policies; and without policies, there is no development. The core of that original vision still holds: either Europe achieves energy independence, or it is destined to surrender. We chose not to drill because it harms the environment. Meanwhile, Russia drilled to supply us with gas, and Arab countries drilled to supply us with oil. We didn't invest in technology because microchips and solar panels were conveniently available from the East at affordable prices. Let's not even get started on batteries. Now, here we are at "Year Zero," and we expect to power everything on electric batteries—even the trendy environmentalist's bicycle. In short, we are bound hand and foot to globalism. And now we're realizing that not only has this left us extremely weak—vulnerable to bad weather, incapable of controlling essential supply chains—but we haven't even succeeded in saving the planet. The countries we've come to depend on are often also the most polluting. Industrial and commercial globalism is a trap. Everyone sees that now. But when someone warned of this years ago, they were accused of being dangerously autarkic. The political challenge today is to have the courage to recognize our mistakes and change course. We must admit that, unlike during the ECSC era, there is no vision guiding us today. Or do we want to keep pretending nothing's wrong and continue with suicidal policies—both in terms of strategic autonomy and autonomy of the environment?

Which policies are you referring to?

Technology and the basic components of a battery-powered world are manufactured in China, mostly in coal-powered plants. The raw materials for their construction—metals and rare elements—are extracted in Africa and—surprise, surprise, once again—in China, often using techniques that are devastating to the environment. Now, they're called *global emissions* for a reason. It doesn't help the planet if Europe imposes drastic measures to reduce harmful emissions, only to outsource production to the Far East, where they use plants that run on coal to produce what you buy. Your ethical choice to pollute less has not solved the planet's problems. You've just weakened your industrial base, you've damaged your economy and, by extension, your social fabric, and you haven't produced any environmental benefits. Take the electric car, for example.

Okay, let's dive in.

A beautiful topic. Who wouldn't want to get behind the wheel of a car that pollutes less—or not at all? No one, I imagine. Is that right? Right. But there's one small detail: if we accelerate the transition too quickly—in other words, if we try to produce electric cars without first building the capability to do so independently—do you know what will happen? In Italy, around 300,000 people will end up living on the street. That's how many workers, directly or indirectly, are linked to the combustion engine sector in Italy. In Germany, the number is even higher. It's estimated that if we stopped producing gas or diesel cars, a million Europeans would no longer have a job. And who would benefit from this? Countries that manufacture electric car components without respecting labor rights or the environmental standards we've set for ourselves. Would global pollution decrease? Obviously not.

Is there a real alternative?

Absolutely—and we've made it one of the key issues for discussion in the European Parliament: we need to find a balance.

With mixed results.

The victory on technological neutrality, however, was largely ours. Without Italy's firm stance on the automotive directive, there wouldn't have even been a debate. Instead, we succeeded—together with countries like Germany—in pushing through the principle that electric is not the only path forward. Gone is the assumption that only electric power qualifies as clean energy—an idea already questionable due to the environmental costs involved in raw material extraction and battery recycling.

What does technological neutrality mean? In essence: the European Union, rightly concerned with environmental issues, sets the goal that by 2035 vehicle emissions must be zero. Correct, I agree. But how each member state reaches that target—that is, through which technology—that should not be dictated by the Commission. Rather, it must be left up to each country's industrial and strategic discretion, so the goal can be met in a way compatible with its own industrial model—and with social sustainability in mind. When it comes to cars, Germany has successfully introduced *e-fuels*—zero-emission synthetic fuels with highly advanced research behind them. In Italy, we're working hard to advance the use of biofuels, thanks largely to our energy company, ENI, and they're just one step away from zero emissions. The point is, you can't tell me today, seeing the speed of technological development, what's going to happen in 2035. If we develop these alternatives, we can preserve our combustion engine–based industry, without compromising environmental goals. Because I have a suspicion—and, as they say, thinking the worst may be a sin, but it's often accurate.

And what suspicions are those?

It's incredible that we don't see how irrational some decisions appear. Often, there's an ideological mindset behind them—a tendency to parrot what others have said rather than verify facts. But I believe there is a huge amount of pressure from certain powerful lobbies influencing these choices. Decisions should be made in the interest of our countries and citizens. So, we must invest in research and believe in our capabilities. For centuries, we Europeans led the world in discoveries and innovations—there's no reason why we can't retain that leadership role.

What we can't do is hand ourselves over to lobbies—or to foreign countries that might use our independence against us, keeping us in their grip economically and therefore politically, as Putin's Russia intended to do the day it decided to invade Ukraine. This is the most important fight that I—and the conservatives—are taking forward in Europe and at every multilateral forum.

I can just hear the objections: "Here comes Meloni the sovereigntist again. . . ."

You can't fight the excesses and distortions of globalism with autarky. That's a biased accusation used by the Left—always quick to attach labels to prop up its shallow narrative, albeit cleverly. The Left's battleground is ideology. Ours, as conservatives, is reality. And reality tells us it's foolish to outsource the production of microchips and semiconductors—now central to every product—outside European borders. What happens is that you lose control. And when you don't control your own fate, any global shock can paralyze you—just as we saw during the COVID-19 pandemic. China prioritized its internal market for chips, and entire European supply chains ground to a halt. You had to wait months—even a year—to buy a new car. Eventually, after a certain delay, Europe tried to solve the problem with the Chips Act, a law that limits its dependence on other countries for these essential components. So, did we make Europe "autarkic"? Or, more simply, did we just face reality? The same pattern played out with the war between Russia and Ukraine, which affected the supply of wheat and fertilizers that are vital to our agriculture. Denying and dismissing these problems as sovereigntist obsessions is not only dishonest—it's a suicidal shortcut.

There's a lot we failed to do—and maybe it's too late to turn things around.

Remember what we used to say? "It's never too late." Or, if you prefer Latin wisdom: "To err is human, but to persist is diabolical." Look, I don't have a magic wand—but I do know this: We're talking about protecting the environment, right? Well then, if Europe wants to implement serious green politics, then it must insist on a baseline of fair conditions in free trade. Because if you trade freely with countries that don't respect your environmental standards, all you'll do is undermine your own system. It may sound banal, but we should remind ourselves more often: civilization and well-being come at a cost. In the West, we have welfare—rights, pensions, maternity leave, minimum wage debate, unemployment benefits, and all the other tools. Do we want to protect all this abundance? If we do, then we must defend it. If, on the one hand, we want to keep these benefits, but on the other, we allow unfair competition from countries that don't share our standards—countries that can sell the same product at prices we can't match—then we're setting up rule-abiding entrepreneurs to fail. Then you're a dead man walking. Doing real green politics means saying loud and clear: *There is no free trade without fair trade*. And this principle must apply across all sectors.

Such as?

Agriculture, for one—the sector most directly tied to the environment. We all know that there are still areas in Italy where workers are illegally hired, underpaid, and exploited—what we call *caporalato*.

The infamous tomato pickers.

Exactly. We continue to pass laws to fight the exploitation of *caporalato* [*the illegal recruiting and organizing of labor,—Translator's Note*] and we're right to be determined in our fight against this barbarism. But then why, under the pretense of "free trade," do we import fruits and vegetables from countries where ethical and social standards are far lower, where exploiting field workers is the rule, not the exception? So, here's my question for those who say I'm an autarkist and a sovereigntist: Why should I be appalled to eat a tomato picked in Italy by some poor guy breaking his back for a few euros a day, while a tomato becomes a delicacy when it's picked by some guy with a broken back a few thousand miles away from us? This is a huge and dangerous hypocrisy because it forces our tomato farmers to choose between shutting down because paying their workers properly would make their tomatoes more expensive than imported ones—meaning that no one would buy them—or underpaying their workers. I want to give this business owner a third option: compete globally with producers who respect their workers as you do—that is, deal with competitors who respect the same rules. Then, yes, may the best producer win.

Maybe I'm missing something, but are you talking about selective imports, or something similar to tariffs in every sector?

What I have in mind is a Europe that's strong and healthy. Within Europe, we can debate and compete among ourselves on various issues—that's what's happening right now with combustion engines and biofuels, and that's entirely fair. But when it comes to relations beyond the Union, we need to reach a shared compromise based on common sense and patience—but also firmness. It's stupid to hold ourselves to impossibly high standards while pretending that the rest of the world doesn't exist. Little by little, we risk exiting the market. Let's set the right rules that align with realistic goals, achievable in credible time frames, by all those involved in global trade. This would lead the change, the famous energy transition with humans inside. Everything else, at best, is ideology. At worst, it's an attempt to colonize us.

A world with humans at its heart—it's a nice recipe. But in the meantime, the world is boiling over, and people risk getting burned. There's a war in the heart of Europe, and who knows how it will end? Maybe sustainable growth isn't a priority right now.

Remember Who We Are

A Lesson from the Ukrainian People

The medical report sounds ominous: today, we start taking antibiotics—this terrible flu is getting out of hand. The thick, white turtleneck beneath her jacket—the outfit Giorgia Meloni wore in the images circulated around the world—did its job, but the long walks, sometimes in the rain and near-freezing temperatures, the day before in Kyiv and its surroundings certainly didn't help her condition. She's visibly tired and under considerable strain, but as always, she downplays anything related to herself. "In these conditions, it's normal to have a slight fever at night," she says. And then: "After what I saw and heard yesterday, complaining about my own problems—big or small—would feel entirely inappropriate."

There. That's what we're talking about. It's February 21, 2023. You go to Kyiv and, I believe for the first time in your life, you step into a war zone.

I arrived and Zelenskyy came to meet me. I had so many thoughts running through my head.

What kind of thoughts?

The kind you might have had yourself; the kind most people would have. Standing before me was a man who found himself facing an immense challenge—possible even one too great—because no one is ever truly ready when history knocks on your door and singles you out. And yet, I believe Zelenskyy proved to be the right man, at the right time, for Ukraine. His critics insist on mentioning his past as a comic actor, as if having a past as an accountant or a lawyer would have been better for confronting the invasion of the Russian army. Might I add that a retired, decorated general turned president would have weighed up the forces in the battlefield and decided that resistance was futile—perhaps that fleeing to safety in the West was the rational choice. Zelenskyy, instead, delivered a line that became a theatrical moment, reported by the Associated Press and worthy of Cyrano: "The fight is here; I need ammunition, not a ride." At that very moment, the entire Ukrainian population identified with its President and decided it would fight the invader, at whatever cost. It defied all logic and common sense.

One officer in our embassy in Ukraine told me that during those days in February 2022, he witnessed the most incredible scenes: men and women in Kyiv preparing to defend their city by any means available to them, some with hunting rifles, makeshift barricades, and even Molotov cocktails to hurl at the Russian army's convoys. No, the Ukrainians were never going to flee, or hide, or surrender. They were going to fight. That's when the course of history changed—not just for Ukraine, but for the whole world. A story that some thought had already been written.

The history of the whole world?

I truly believe that. The Ukrainian resistance was an unexpected turning point in history. Remember the movie *Sliding Doors*? Remember how the main character's life changes radically because of a simple, seemingly insignificant choice? In this case, the Ukrainian's unpredictable doggedness—and its people's heroic response—was the sliding doors moment that changed the course of history. A black swan event no analyst had predicted. The Kremlin had planned for Ukraine to capitulate within a few days. It certainly didn't expect the country to resist—and even launch a counteroffensive to reclaim occupied territories.

What kind of future would we have had without this black swan and if Russia had gained a swift victory?

We'd have a Ukraine invaded, broken apart, and used as a springboard to attack other European nations. Let's rewind for a moment. Does anyone seriously believe Ukraine was invaded because it talked about joining NATO? Or to protect Russian-speaking minorities allegedly oppressed by Kyiv? Even Yevgeny Prigozhin, head of the Wagner group, admitted those claims were ridiculous lies spread by Russian propaganda. Did you know that Russians make up less than 40 percent of Donbas's population? Ukrainians are the majority. But the Kremlin's propaganda claims otherwise. Just as it deliberately conflated *Russophones*—Ukrainians who also speak Russian—with ethnic Russians. Confusing the two is misleading—and, unfortunately, it's something I've heard from otherwise respected commentators. A part of Belgium speaks French, but no one would seriously suggest that this legitimizes a French invasion to annex territories and defend "Francophones." Let's not fall into that trap. The invasion of Ukraine must be understood within a broader context—part of a pattern we've seen before: Crimea and Donbas in 2014, and before that in Georgia and Moldova . . . It's a plan for renewed Russian expansionism.

Putin as a tsar.

Put like that, it may make you grin—but it's not far from the truth. Do you know what tsars are remembered for in Russian history? For two things, essentially: the territories they conquered and the ones they lost. Putin inherited a country that, after the dissolution of the USSR, was at its lowest territorial extent in centuries.

But he wants to be remembered . . .

Exactly. By rebuilding the great Russia of old. We may not have paid close attention at the time, but on many occasions, Putin spoke of restoring Russia's historical borders. That includes not only Ukraine but also Moldova, Estonia, Latvia, Lithuania—and even much of Finland. He was just waiting for the right time to act on a vision he had long held.

The right time—what time?

August 31, 2021. That was the watershed moment: the day the West hastily withdrew from Afghanistan, leaving the country—and its people—in the hands of the Taliban. It was a clear sign of weakness. I said so then, and I repeat it now: the enemies of the West understood that moment instantly.

At the time, you criticized President Biden's Democratic administration harshly: "It couldn't have done much worse." But the decision to withdraw from Afghanistan was made by Trump in 2020.

Actually, it was announced even earlier by Barack Obama. But it's one thing to withdraw in an orderly fashion after twenty years, and another to flee live on TV. I think all of us remember those chilling images of the airport in Kabul under siege—women and children, desperate for a pass to freedom and salvation, after trusting the West to protect them from the fury of the Taliban. The fact is, that day the whole world saw just how fragile the West was. Russia reared its ugly head, and China took a more assertive stance toward Taiwan.

They must have thought: If the West looks weak, then we should take advantage of it . . .

And if Ukraine had surrendered, that thought would've been validated. From the very next day, other countries might have found themselves in the crosshairs of expansionist powers, both large and medium-sized.

On September 18, 2018, ANSA—the Italian national press agency—reported a leaked document published by the German daily newspaper Süddeutsche Zeitung, *based on EU diplomatic sources. The report claimed that Putin had threatened then–Ukrainian President Petro Porošenko: "If I wanted, Russian troops could be not only in Kyiv, but also in Riga, Vilnius, Tallinn, Warsaw, and Bucharest in two days."*

I remember, and I wasn't surprised. Let me put it plainly, so everyone can understand: Today it's Ukraine. Tomorrow, it could be any territory Russia claims as its own. It should come as no surprise that Russian troops entered Ukraine waving flags emblazoned with the hammer and sickle. This is Soviet imperial nostalgia.

Do you really believe that Russia could ever attack a NATO member?

Let's think this through. Imagine a future in which Ukraine has fallen, and Russia launches another disinformation campaign—like we've already seen in Georgia and Ukraine. It's easy to imagine Russian propaganda declaring: "Russian minorities are being discriminated against in Lithuania, Latvia, and Estonia. We must intervene to defend our Russian brothers." What happens if, one day, Russia invades one of these countries, with Moscow claiming that a "Russophobic Nazi regime" is committing genocide against Russian minorities? Would NATO invoke the famous Article 5, which treats an attack on one member state as an attack on the entire alliance—even if that means risking open conflict between NATO and the Russian Federation? Or even World War III involving nuclear warheads?

If the West shows weakness in the invasion of Ukraine, then yes, Russia might risk attacking a NATO state. But let's put it this way: I'd rather not find out. Ukraine's victory in a conventional war could prevent Russia from venturing into a new war by invasion. And it could also temper any imperialist ambitions of other global powers, medium or large. It's simple: if we accept a world where international law is replaced by the law of the strongest, then, starting tomorrow, we'll all be living in a far more dangerous, unstable place. Europe—and Italy—stand to lose the most. That's why I'm convinced that Ukraine is fighting for *us* as well. Its resistance distances us from a world war—it doesn't bring us closer to one. Supporting Ukraine means working for peace. Exactly the opposite of what some voices in Italy claim, misleading the public for the sole purpose of getting votes.

Is that why you wanted to go to Kyiv? What did Zelenskyy ask of you?

I remember Zelenskyy approaching me in his military fatigues—the ones we've all grown used to seeing. And I was struck by the fact that some people have even found a way to criticize what he wears. Apparently, there are some who believe a true leader, even during a war, while his people are under fire by bombs and missiles, should still wear a suit and tie—or even a tuxedo in the evening—instead of an army sweater. He gets straight to the point, there's no room for rhetoric. Just a few words, no small talk. Then he takes a piece of paper from his pocket and says, "Giorgia, sorry—you have this . . ."

Have what?

Electric generators, spare parts, antiaircraft defense—it doesn't matter what. I instantly knew that I was standing in front of someone who is solely focused on saving his people, who is aware of everything that is needed, down to the smallest detail, and that piece of paper was the proof. It's humbling to find yourself faced with a simple reality: when you're in the middle of a storm—or a war—every single machinery component can mean the difference between life and death for many. But the thing that most struck me about that visit wasn't my meeting with Zelenskyy.

What was it?

Small but revealing things about the atmosphere and the expectations placed on us. When I got to my hotel in Kyiv, I got to my room and found a piece of paper on the table. I kept it, and still remember what it said: "Thank you for what you're doing for us, for our cause, for our freedom, for our sovereignty." Signed: the hotel manager. Then I went to Bucha and along the way, I saw a sign by the road that read: "Thank you, Italy, for what you are doing for us." And between one stop and another, they showed me pictures.

Pictures of what?

That very morning, about sixty miles from where we were, the Russians had attacked and killed six civilians who were out shopping. The photos showed the people who had lost their lives. And seeing their bodies—their expressions, their unnatural poses—make the difference when you're trying to understand the atrocities of war. It's like looking at a picture of someone who may even be smiling—but who is no longer alive. I first experienced this at the Holocaust Museum in Israel. When you get to the last room, the walls are covered with close-up portraits of the people murdered by the fury of the Nazis. That's when it hits you: war and barbarity are not just political issues, they're not abstract concepts far away from you. And the victims aren't just numbers—though we always remember the statistics. They are individual lives, individual faces. They have names, they could be your brother, your father, your son. Time stood still in front of those stuffed animals placed on the graves of the children of Bucha. Its mayor gave me a medal inscribed with the words: *An unconquered city.*

All the more reason for the war to end as soon as possible.

You don't need to tell me that. I would want this war to end today. Peace is a precious asset that must be safeguarded when you have it, and pursued with everything you've got when you've lost it. But I also believe this: you cannot achieve solid, long-lasting peace unless it is also a just peace. This isn't anything new. The concept of a just peace and a just war have been part of European thought since Aristotle and Cicero, and is deeply rooted in Catholic doctrine. Can you really call it a peace when it means surrendering to invaders? To those who take your freedom by force? Sincerely, I don't think so. I don't share the view of certain self-styled intellectuals in our country who say, "A child can be happy even in a dictatorship," or, "It's better to live under tyranny than to die resisting it." These are ideas that have been repeated, in various forms, by our pacifists and by those who argue we should stop supporting Ukraine. I see it differently. Freedom always comes at a price—sometimes a very high one. But the true greatness of a person, and of a people, can be measured precisely by the price they are willing to pay for their freedom.

There are those who say that the West wants to fight Russia to the last Ukrainian.

Yes, I've heard that too—just one of the many reasons some use to justify abandoning Ukraine. First, we were told we shouldn't support Ukraine because it's too weak. Then, because it's too strong. First, people said the Ukrainians don't deserve support because of their many "faults," then they shouldn't be helped for their own good because doing so would only lead them to die fighting "to the last Ukrainian," as you said. What some in the West struggle to accept is that Ukrainians will fight no matter what—for their land and for their freedom, with or without our help. Ukrainians possess what I can only define as "heroic resignation." When you speak to them, they tell you they have no choice. It is neither recklessness nor fearlessness. It's the awareness that they must do what is right. And they're willing to accept the consequences.

When the war began, thousands of Russians fled abroad to avoid conscription. In those same days, thousands of Ukrainians from around the world returned to their homeland to fight: athletes, artists, singers, students. Many stories have stayed with me. Among them is the story of a young woman, Marianna Triasko, an Italian of Ukrainian origin, wife, and mother of two children aged ten and fourteen. She left Treviso and joined the army as a military medic. She died on the front lines, about twelve miles from the nuclear power plant of Zaporizhzhia. Defending her country came before everything else.

But what drives Ukrainians isn't just "love of country." When you ask them why they fight, almost all have the same reply: "We want to give our children a better future than the one we had under Russian rule." And with this knowledge, they are determined and serene. They showed me a video of three Ukrainian youths—one of them a girl—riding in a Ukrainian armored car, the soundtrack of *Dirty Dancing* blaring as they raced into battle. They had hope, they laughed, they sang. I don't know if they were seeking "a good death." What's certain is that if they did die, then they wanted to die happy. That was the moment I understood: this war would never be resolved through political negotiations that ignore the will of the Ukrainian people and their desire for freedom.

That's why Putin couldn't break them—not by bombing their cities, striking their power stations to plunge them into cold and darkness, not by destroying their churches and monuments, nor through the brutal violence his troops inflict on civilians. Maybe the reason so many in the West are divided over Ukraine is because the Ukrainians' extraordinary resilience forces us to remember something we've forgotten—what we Europeans once were.

What do you mean by that?

If I tell you, you'll think I'm crazy.

I know you're the Prime Minister, but I'll take the risk.

Have you noticed how closely what's happening in Ukraine mirrors some of the most defining events in our own history? Look at the epic ancient siege of Bakhmut—fought house by house, keeping thousands of Russians mired for months and months, preventing them from advancing on other cities. Or consider the incredible resistance of the Azovstal iron and steel works in Mariupol. It recalls the Battle of Thermopylae: surrounded from the very start of the war, and yet the resistance held out for three months, buying the Ukrainian army time to regroup.

Pure epic. A year later came the revenge. According to legend, Dilios—heir to Leonidas, king of the Spartans slain at Thermopylae—said this before the final battle: "Remember us." As simple an order as a king can give. "Remember why we died."

That's right. And the entire Greek world—that is, the ancient Western world (another similarity)—rushed to stand by Sparta's side to defeat the Persian invaders. Let's set aside the mythology and legends. That line—"Remember why we died"—is absolutely true of Ukraine today. *We are a sovereign people. We are a free nation and want to remain one. We are willing to die for that.* I wish we could say the same for ourselves: Remember why we died. Remember that our civilization was born of this courage.

The polls suggest otherwise.

I'm well aware. Most Italians believe this war doesn't concern them and would rather look the other way. What disappoints me is that this attitude doesn't only include the heirs of the Left—those who, during the Cold War, were paid by the Kremlin to push pacifist ideas—but also those from the history of the Right. Some of them, in good faith, see Russia as an alternative to the "decadence of the West." But in the words of the philosopher Marcello Pera—currently a senator of Brothers of Italy and an intellectual who has never held back from criticizing the West—the road to reviving our civilization does not involve looking to Putin's regime, which has nothing to teach us. It means going back to our foundational values. As I see it, those values are freedom, democracy, equality, the sanctity of human life, the centrality of the individual. Values that are distant from what Russia represents today.

Yet, many are calling for diplomacy to intervene.

That's right, and we're working on that around the clock. We need to find a way to end this war in a way that does not allow Russia to take over Ukraine. That's precisely why, to support diplomatic efforts, we must help Ukraine.

Put like that, it sounds like an oxymoron.

It seems like one, but it isn't. As we've seen, the Ukrainians' most powerful weapon is their strength of will. Yet, their weakness is their material inferiority to the enemy. The only diplomatic way forward, to get the two sides to sit down around a table, is to create a balance of power on the battlefield. The reasoning is simple: If Putin is convinced Ukraine will eventually surrender, why should he ever agree to sit down at a negotiating table? Why negotiate after losing huge numbers of men and resources? He'd rather keep going, waiting, continuing his war of aggression. Victory on the battlefield is his preferred—and so far, only—option.

Your explanation is clear and simple, but nonetheless, these are complicated issues. It's not easy to break through the public's wall of fear. Their argument is even more simple: Let's end it now and deal with the consequences later. You talk of matters that seem distant in time and space.

The problem is, these "distant things" are much closer than we think—both in time and space. I was struck by something Paolo, one of my collaborators, told me. Just days after February 24, as he left home for work—his usual routine, a day like any other—he noticed a family at the entrance to his building: a mother, father, and three children—one nearly a teenager, the others younger. They were bundled up, carrying bags and suitcases. They had a lost look in their eyes. One little girl wore a red scarf around her neck and Minnie Mouse earmuffs. At first, he thought nothing of it, but when he asked his neighbors who they were, he learned they were a Ukrainian family—refugees, fleeing the bombs, taken in by a relative who lived in Paolo's building. "Giorgia," he told me, his eyes filled with tears, "at that moment, the war entered my own home. It was a gut punch. . . ." Paolo has three kids, and he must have seen his own family in those children, in that mother and father. The war in Ukraine concerns all of us, it touches us all. That's the message.

Aren't you afraid of being misunderstood?

I'm going to give it my all to be understood. That said, there's one thing I won't budge on. I will always do what is useful and right for my country—even if it means losing public support.

I'm trying to imagine where you want to position yourself. . . .

I stand where Italy's interests are. Always. I only make decisions based on what I believe is right for Italians. And in the case of Ukraine, I have no doubt. Even if we set aside moral obligations, even if we set aside our admiration for Ukrainian bravery, let's think about it in practical terms. Italy is part of a complex network of international alliances that guarantees its security and supports our economy through trade. Do people really think that if Italy were to suddenly pull out of the game today, confirming its image as an unreliable country—all "spaghetti and mandolins"—it would not damage our international credibility and future relations with partners? Obviously, it would, and the cost would be very high. We would be weaker, more vulnerable to danger, and we would be less welcome to participate in trade agreements. And for what? All this without having influenced the outcome of the war (as I'm not sure our aid is crucial for Ukraine). Those who argue we should not honor our international alliances are nothing short of geopolitical self-sabotage. I'm certain of that: the only way to protect Italy is to prove that we are a reliable partner. The more credible you are, the more weight your voice carries at the negotiating table. That's how you protect your values.

Loyal to NATO and the EU?

I would say loyal to Italy. That's the only thing that interests me. However, I'm forced to point out that since World War II, no Western country—except those with historic neutrality—has done without a military or an international network of alliances.

Some might argue that defense comes at a price. Can we afford it?

Freedom has a cost. Independence has a cost. Being taken seriously on an international level comes with a cost. But the price you pay is far lower than the advantages you can draw from being a credible part of a multilateral system. It's significantly more expensive to be at the mercy of world events because of your own weakness and irrelevance.

Still, the most heated debate isn't about weapons to defend Italy; it's about sending weapons to Ukraine, both because of the expense and the political decisions.

Much of what we've done for Ukraine involves protecting civilians: generators, ambulances, and medical aid. Weapons too, of course—primarily de-mining tools, anti-missile systems, and air defense equipment. When it comes to the cost, let's clarify things: today, I'm not spending money to buy weapons to send to Ukraine. I already have a defense stock, and I am transferring some of it to Ukraine. I'm not pulling money away from food banks—as some naively suggest. No, that's not how it works. We're talking about money that's already been spent on defense. We're talking about resources, munitions, tools that we already have at our disposal.

Even so, the accusation is misleading because, as the government has already stated in Parliament, there's no direct link between what we've sent and what we need to restock. These transfers are part of long-term planning and the acquisition of new equipment is independent of these transfers to Ukraine. In addition, we're fortunate to not currently need these resources for our own direct defense. In fact, in the medium- to long term, this equipment would reach the end of its technical lifespan, and would have to be scrapped and replaced anyway. In short, I believe that our efforts are more than justified in contributing to the defense of international rights and our own national interests.

Someone—I can't recall who—said: "Without a clear foreign policy you can't have an effective domestic policy." Do you agree?

I don't know who said that, but they were definitely wise.

Head Held High Among the World Greats

Traveling with Hello Kitty

Today we're on an outing, just a few hundred feet away from Palazzo Chigi, at the Chamber of Deputies in the wing reserved for parliamentary groups. Here, on the sixth floor, is Giorgia Meloni's hideaway, where she holes up when she needs to work without feeling like she's at the office. To reach her secret office, you navigate a maze of corridors and ride several elevators up and down. It's said to be the nicest office in the entire Chamber, one she chose years ago when Brothers of Italy was still a very small party, and she has not given it up since. The room itself is small—which is probably why other parties let her have it, not understanding what they were giving up—but the view is vast, grand even. You can see all of Rome from here, so close you could almost touch it. At this time of day, with the sun having just set and the city lights aglow, it doesn't just *look* magical, it *is* magical. A shame we have to turn away from the view and get down to work.

In the words of Confucius in the fifth century BC: "To put the world in order, we must first put the nation in order; to put the nation in order, we must put the family in order; to put the family in order, we must cultivate our personal life; and to cultivate our personal life, we must first set our hearts right." Madame Prime Minister, do you agree?

Well, let's just say that ancient wisdom still holds true. Even twenty-five centuries later, it reads like an excellent plan for governance. I agree, essentially, that everything must be connected within a consistent political and cultural vision. You can't take a little from here and a little from there. Your policy line has to be the same whether you're talking to evicted tenants about housing or to the President of the United States about crucial geopolitical issues.

I know you spoke at length with President Biden—we'll come back to that in a moment—but first, what are your thoughts on foreign policy?

What used to annoy me was seeing so many Italian leaders—including Prime Ministers and party secretaries—trying to imitate or even win the approval of foreign leaders, as though that alone could make them important. So of course, people started trying to assign *me* a foreign label. Do you know how many times I've been called a "Trumper," an "Orbanist," a "LePenist"? I've always found it childish and provincial. First, because if you're busy trying to look or act like someone else, then you're not a leader. And second, because needing a foreign model reflects a certain inferiority complex—a very Italian one. You don't see this ridiculous debate happening in other countries. And if models are really that important, then my goal is to create an original one, not import or copy one. We are Italy, for heaven's sake.

So you're saying you're essentially "Melonian."

I realize that it might not be the most marketable name, but yes—that's definitely the definition that fits best.

Some have even said you're "Draghian." But let's try to define this "Melonism."

More than being a Draghian, they claim I'm implementing Draghi's agenda. But if you ask those people what the Draghi agenda actually is, they won't have an answer. In fact, Mario Draghi himself said, "It's hard to say that a Draghi agenda even exists." Which says a lot about how, in Italy, we sometimes debate for months without knowing what we're debating about, simply because it's a catchy headline. In any case, Melonism, as you call it, in foreign policy, boils down to one simple concept: to always pursue Italy's national interests. Regardless of whom you're talking to, where they're from, their political orientation, their power, or personal dynamics with you.

The Minister of the Economy Giorgetti confessed that he was impressed by your meeting with President Xi Jinping of China.

It was a one-on-one bilateral that lasted over an hour.

It was November 16, 2022. You had been Prime Minister just a few weeks. Bali, Indonesia—your first G20, the intergovernmental forum with all the world's greats. You arrived wearing a dark jacket and skirt, your hair in a ponytail, and you sat down with—arguably—the most powerful person on the planet.

Yes, the very man. We were in a vast hall adorned with Italian and Chinese flags. Observers said it might have been a gesture of kindness toward Italy, but it definitely had a slightly intimidating air. My views on Chinese politics are well-known—and they're not always positive—and I imagine President Xi was aware of them. But he was gracious and attentive, proof of the solid relations that the Dragon and the *Belpaese*—our beautiful country—have enjoyed for centuries. I was equally pleasant with him. We discussed cooperation and culture, as is natural between the heirs to civilizations that stretch back thousands of years. That shared depth is a key point of contact between Italy and China. Then, halfway through our talk, we got down to brass tacks. We are both forthright, and I believe real relationships cannot grow from hypocrisy. I brought up human rights; his body stiffened. Then we turned to trade, and he raised concerns about what he sees as excessive restrictions. But I pointed out that, in recent years, Italian exports to China have grown by just a few percentage points, while Chinese exports to Italy have grown significantly more. In other words, it became a cordial but intense back-and-forth. It was very interesting, very real.

When it came time to say goodbye, Xi smiled again. I thought, like me, he appreciates people who are sincere. That's why I left the meeting feeling more optimistic than when I walked in—even though it was pretty hard work. At any rate, as we were leaving, Giancarlo Giorgetti came up beside me and said, "Hmmm, well done." Then I saw him quietly slip out of the building.

The official news was that Xi was very satisfied and that he invited you to Beijing to continue the conversation.

Yes, we parted with the understanding that I would lead a mission to China, and I intend to honor that promise. Every first encounter is like laying the first brick in a relationship—and, in foreign affairs, good relationships are everything. But to build something real, you have to speak honestly. And I believe that with countries like China—but also with North African nations, and more broadly, with Arab-speaking ones, who have little tolerance for Western hypocrisy—this forthrightness pays off. When I first met President Saied of Tunisia, he said to me, in front of the cameras: "You are a woman who has the courage to say out loud what everyone else is thinking." It's a sentiment that I've heard from other leaders in different forms. Being frank means not evading problems, avoiding misunderstandings, openly stating your objectives. It also means asking your counterpart what their objectives are so that we can understand how to find common ground. Because the other thing that's fundamental in our relationships with these countries is respect—especially rejecting the paternalistic attitude we've seen too often in the past. That condescension of those who look down on others while still expecting them to solve their problems. Here's an example. Patrick Zaki, the young Egyptian student in Bologna who was detained in Egypt. When he was sentenced and then pardoned by the Egyptian President al-Sisi within twenty-four hours, allowing him to return to Italy, many claimed that this outcome was part of some trade-off—gas deals or who knows what else. But that's not true. Nothing was "exchanged" for Patrick Zaki—except for mutual respect between us and the Egyptian president.

How is your approach different from that of previous governments?

I've heard of Italian politicians who were conciliatory in private but then postured aggressively in public, playing to the crowd. I believe the opposite is better. You must have the courage to say difficult things, especially when it's just the two of you. Because if you attack a partner publicly, when you deny them respect, you shouldn't expect them to appreciate you. And if a door slams in your face, if there's a price, it's not the politician who pays it—it's the nation.

But people have tried to slam doors on you too, several times. France comes to mind, but also the Prime Minister of Canada at the G7 in Japan, who publicly expressed concern about gay rights in Italy.

And the very next day he came to apologize. In the heat of the moment, I asked him what exactly he was concerned about. What worried him, given that the government had not taken up any legislative initiatives on the issue of gay rights? The truth is, he couldn't be specific. He had simply expressed a general concern. In the hours that followed, we gave each other the cold shoulder. But then Trudeau must have realized his mistake. He had been misled by fake news circulated by a certain news outlet that, astonishingly, made its way around the world. He saw firsthand, over the course of long meetings at the G7, that the person described to him in media reports was quite different from the one in the room. In any case, we cleared things up—but the episode speaks volumes about the way we are stigmatized.

Stigmatized or not, the impression is that you are respected as a leader.

I believe I have an advantage over my recent predecessors. For years, whenever an Italian head of government or a minister sat down with a foreign partner, the first question on that counterpart's mind was more or less: "Will I be dealing with the same Italian official at our next meeting?" More often than not, by the time the next meeting rolled around, the Italian government had changed. This lack of continuity has been devastating for our foreign policy. Serious relationships and strategic choices require time. My advantage—aside from speaking English, Spanish, and a bit of French, which allows for immediate and empathetic personal interaction that becomes impossible when talking through an interpreter—is time. When counterparts sit across from us now, they know there's a good chance they'll be speaking to the same people again at the next meeting. That makes them more invested in building a good relationship, and much more open to discussing strategic collaborations. After all, foreign policy is about understanding and agreements. When a government falls, the agreements it was working on often collapse, too. That's one of the reasons Italy has been considered unreliable on the world stage.

The infamous "Italietta," little Italy.

That's why I believe government stability isn't just a simple whim—it's one of the most powerful economic assets Italy can have. I've set myself the goal of serving a full term. Not because I want to stay glued to my seat for five years, but because it's the only way to give Italy real influence in the world. And let me add this: I'm working with a vision that extends beyond these five years. I hope that whoever comes after me won't feel the need to tear everything down. I can't guarantee how things will go—it's not all up to me—but I know this is a unique opportunity for this country in a very difficult situation, and I will do everything in my power not to waste it.

Italians may not realize just how much the constant government turnover has cost us. On the international level—as we've seen within the European Union—what counts is the relationships you build, the trust you earn, the seriousness you project, the person you are. What counts is being the kind of partner who helps others when they're in trouble, and in turn, receives help when needed. And this takes time. When I read snide comments in the newspapers about the supposed lack of results after just one foreign mission, I can't help but smile. These relationships are like any human relationship: they require patience and time. I give it my all, and I know only the facts will prove whether I'm the serious person I claim to be. I'm perfectly aware of this. Just as I'm aware that—if and when I pass the test—the real fruits of this hard work will begin to show.

Personal relationships—something you're clearly focused on.

Do you really believe that the dynamics at the highest levels of politics are so different from those in everyday life? Of course not. What matters, for example, is how comfortable people feel with you, how much you succeed in stepping into their world, understanding them, putting yourself in their shoes and responding to their needs. Every country has its own history, and almost every leader is trying to do what's best for their people—or at least what sounds best to their public. It's the same for everyone: If you don't ask what you can do to help others, you can't expect them to help in return. The key is that the relationship must be one of equals. On the subject of personal relationships, it's important to move beyond rigid formality, of the rules of behavior, and to find your personal key. A few witty words, a personal story, a common interest—it can make all the difference. I regret to admit that I've started smoking again after thirteen years, though I've built some solid diplomatic relationships over a cigarette break. I often think back to my first meeting with Tunisian President Saied. He's a man of strong character and a skilled negotiator. During my visit to Tunisia, our bilateral meeting lasted almost two hours. Afterward, he took me to see the view of the ocean from his beautiful home. I asked hesitantly, "Mr. President, would you mind if I smoked?" He was overjoyed! He pulled out his own pack of cigarettes, and that coffee and cigarette break became our moment.

Even a little healthy irony—especially self-irony—can go a long way in breaking down barriers. For example, British Prime Minister Rishi Sunak and I once sent a video to Giancarlo Giorgetti—who, don't ask me why—is a Southampton soccer fan. It was the day I was in London and the team was about to play a very important game.

Many were intrigued by a picture of you and Sunak laughing, both looking at something on a phone.

Rishi and I are friends—we're practically the same age, and we were both elected around the same time. We're both conservatives, we support each other, and we each represent a "first" for our countries: I'm Italy's first female Prime Minister, and he's the first British Prime Minister whose parents were immigrants. In any case, you won't believe me, but I was showing him a picture of the Italian singer Orietta Berti.

Orietta Berti?

Yes! We were at the NATO summit's social dinner in Vilnius, and I was wearing a very sparkly outfit. Before heading out, I'd been on a video call with Andrea, who teased me, saying I reminded him a little of Orietta Berti. I don't know why, but I started telling Sunak about it. He asked, "Who's Orietta Berti?" So I pulled up a photo of the singer—whom I adore—wearing a sequined dress.

Any other anecdotes?

With Mohammed bin Zayed, President of the United Arab Emirates—our relationship with the UAE has been strained, but we were able to heal things. It really solidified over an informal lunch in a Japanese restaurant in Abu Dhabi—he even drove me there himself, as if we were old friends. A similar thing happened with the Ethiopian Prime Minister Abiy Ahmed Ali. He also drove me, this time around Addis Ababa, on a long tour of major infrastructure projects he had built in record time. Along the way, we shared stories about our respective careers.

Edi Rama also comes to mind, Prime Minister of Albania. He speaks perfect Italian, follows our politics closely, and we often exchange messages about current events. Edi is one of the most fun and spontaneous people I've ever met.

Serbian President Aleksandar Vučić is a great connoisseur of Italian wines, and for my birthday, he sent me a splendid bouquet of orange roses. Japanese Prime Minister Fumio Kishida is also a fan of Italian wines. When we met at the G7 in Hiroshima, he gave me a giant Hello Kitty doll for Ginevra.

When I visited Warsaw, Polish Prime Minister Mateusz Morawiecki—knowing how much I love Tolkien—took me for a coffee at a café themed after *The Lord of the Rings*. We stood there talking about a huge, gorgeous map of Middle-earth.

And I'll never forget President Shavkat Mirziyoyev of Uzbekistan. Before our bilateral meeting in Rome, he had my previous book, *I Am Giorgia*, translated into Uzbek so he could read it. He brought me a bound copy of it. What I want to say is this: just as I remember the personal side of my relationships with world leaders, I believe they do, too. We're all human beings playing a game that often feels much bigger than we are. And in that context, a personal relationship can ease the pressure and help you truly understand the person in front of you.

They say that when you visited India this past March, there were posters with your face everywhere in New Delhi.

That's right. When I arrived, there was a poster with my face and the word *Welcome* every few feet along the road. When I left, the posters showed the same image, but now read *Thank you for visiting.* My colleague Antonio Tajani, who was with me, joked: "With all these posters, if you ran for the New Delhi constituency, you'd get a million votes."

Let's move to what your critics call the most sensitive issue: your relationship with the United States of America, represented by President Joe Biden today, which is described as being too complacent.

You might think it sounds presumptuous, but I don't have an inferiority complex—regardless of whom I'm dealing with. Not because I think I'm important, but because I represent a country that is. So, I feel just as free and at ease with Joe Biden as I do before Xi Jinping. I'm fully aware of the differences in clout and scale, but I don't believe I need to please anyone—not even America. Are they our allies? Of course they are, but a serious ally is someone who can disagree with you honestly. Others may think they're doing Italy a favor by saying yes to everything, only to act differently behind the scenes. I prefer to say no when I must—and I often do—but you can be sure of one thing: I will never deceive you. For me, it's always about one thing: Italy's national interest. And I always declare this up front when I meet with a foreign leader.

They say I'm soft on the Americans because I've been one of the strongest supporters of Ukraine in the war, and that I do it to ensure US support—though for what, exactly, I'm not sure. But those making that claim forget that I held that very same position when I was in the opposition. Because I always make decisions based on what I believe in, not out of political calculation.

Critics say that the US is only pursuing its own interests.

Of course! America looks after its own interests, but that doesn't mean that they can't be aligned with ours. It's normal for them to do so—the real question is whether we are pursuing ours with the same conviction. And this also means recognizing when—despite the US being our historical, solid ally—our interests overlap or not, whether those of Italy and the US, or Europe and the US. For example, prior to February 24, 2022, I don't regret having supported the idea of working toward a lasting peace with Russia to prevent it from forming an alliance with China. Then Putin invaded Ukraine, and everything changed. Of course, when it comes to the US, the situation is more complicated. It would be an oversimplification to reduce it to the case of Ukraine.

What do you mean by that?

What I mean is that rather than focusing solely on America and what it does—often legitimately—we should reflect on what Europe has or hasn't done. The two must be considered together; otherwise the discussion is half-baked. Let me explain. First, it's undeniable that, in the aftermath of World War II, parts of Europe avoided fully assuming their responsibilities for far too long, failing to build the capacity to defend themselves independently. After all, there was always someone—namely, the United States—acting as a "protective father." But, as I've said many times before, including here, it's naive to think you can rely on others to pay for your defense and security without them expecting something in return. It's no coincidence that Brothers of Italy is the only political force that has consistently had the courage to include increased defense spending in its political platform—not because we like weapons, but because investing in defense is the foundation for asserting and protecting your national interests. The second issue lies entirely within Europe: what's been lacking is strong, generous and balanced leadership.

Can you elaborate?

The United Kingdom has always charted its own course, due in part to historical reasons and its close ties with the Americans—eventually choosing and having the strength to leave the European Union while still maintaining a balanced alliance with the US. Within the EU, Germany and France have leveraged their power and long-established alliance to pursue their own interests—including geopolitical ones—sometimes disregarding the other member states. Just think of the special relationship between Germany and Russia, which rightly raised concerns in Eastern European countries. The invasion of Ukraine confirmed that those fears were justified. It's only natural, then, that these nations sought support elsewhere. And where, if not on the other side of the Atlantic? Of course, these Eastern countries, once Soviet satellites, feel safer leaning on Washington than on Berlin or Paris. And no one in Europe offered them a real alternative. On the contrary, relations with countries like Poland and Hungary, for example, were further strained by a particularly hostile stance toward them.

In short, the Franco-German bloc hasn't always served as a balanced reference point for everyone, large or small, allies and non-allies alike. It's clear that this void has allowed American influence in Europe to grow. Similarly, the lack of a clear European strategy on many sensitive fronts—from supply chains onward—has made us vulnerable, playing right into the hands of the United States.

And that still holds today?

I'll be generous: first the pandemic, then the conflict in Ukraine, opened our eyes to just how much had been swept under the rug. But Europe is still not changing enough, nor at the necessary speed. Take strategic decisions, for example. Americans responded to inflationary pressure with the Inflation Reduction Act, a $370 billion investment package aimed at strengthening their economic and energy security. In Europe, we spent months discussing how to respond to the risk of investments relocating abroad, but we have yet to find any decisive solutions. Some member states oppose the idea of a strategic sovereign fund, while others reject even recognizing investments in green and digital transitions under the new Stability and Growth Pact rules. We are finally acknowledging the problems, but our response remains too slow and insufficiently bold. When it comes to major strategic decisions, those with the most clout still tend to act in their own interest, rather than from a truly European perspective.

Basically, a holistic vision is lacking.

In foreign policy, vision is everything. And, at the risk of sounding presumptuous, I believe what sets Italy apart today is precisely that we have a political government—one with a clear vision that brings real substance to international discussions. We are listened to and respected because we have something to say.

We've highlighted the importance of building equal partnerships with African nations and emphasized the central role of the Mediterranean—and more broadly, of maritime strategy—with a focus on the opportunities the Indo-Pacific can offer, especially for Italian entrepreneurs. Just to give you an example: did you know that, thanks to the expansion of the Suez Canal, it's now easier for goods to reach Italy from India than from Norway? The relationship with Latin America also deserves to be nurtured, and that's my next area of focus. Italian communities abroad have long preceded our diplomatic efforts there, and the bonds are so strong that our entrepreneurs often say it's easier to do business in Uruguay, Chile, and Mexico than in some European countries. What we need is a vision—and lots of hard work. Vision and work go hand in hand.

The most famous vision is that of turning Italy into the Mediterranean hub—the energy crossroads for all of Europe.

The Mattei Plan; not a random name.

Yes, indeed. Enrico Mattei—a "white partisan" during the Resistance—was appointed in 1945 as the liquidator of AGIP, the oil company founded under the fascist regime. But instead of shutting it down, he defied expectations and transformed it into ENI, which went on to literally fuel the Italian economic miracle of the 1960s.

That's the story in short. But the name Mattei still evokes two other ideas that remain highly relevant today. The first is that Mattei wanted energy independence. He challenged the "Seven Sisters"—the seven major oil companies around the world that operated under the tight control of the United States and the United Kingdom. So much for autonomy. The second is his approach to Africa. He sought oil and gas there, yes, but unlike others, he paid close attention to the economic and human needs of the nations and peoples with whom he signed agreements. Some say that because of both these things, someone—whose identity remains unknown to this day—may have had him killed by causing his private plane to crash near Milan on the evening of October 27, 1962, as he returned from a business trip to Sicily.

I hope the same fate doesn't befall me [*laughs*], but the fact remains: several African nations consider him a hero. Streets and plaques bearing his name still exist today, sixty years later. That must signify something. Just think, in Algiers, there's even a public garden named after Mattei—not because he discovered gas fields there, but because he supported Algeria in its war for independence from colonial rule. Mattei believed in Africa's development and in the rights of its peoples to prosper through the resources of their land. Because Africa is not poor at all—it's exploited.

And you see, there are two ways to approach development cooperation. There are those who, when there's no water, bring you bottled water. And there are those who bring you a desalination plant to make seawater drinkable. In other words, there are those who use aid to foster dependence, and those who use development to foster independence. I believe in the second model. The Mattei Plan for Africa is built on this principle. The goal is to invest in African energy production—especially clean, renewable energy—which means development for them, and energy autonomy for both sides. It's that simple.

Please explain.

Just take a look at the map of the Mediterranean. Italy sits right at the center—between those who can extract or produce energy, both traditional and renewable (thanks to favorable climates), and those who lack energy but desperately need it. In other words, we are geographically positioned to act as a bridge between Africa and Northern, Central, and Eastern Europe. The Mattei Plan seeks to connect this supply with that demand, and Italy is the ideal—almost natural—platform to serve as a hub for energy sourcing and distribution.

I've emphasized this point many times, including at the Raisina Dialogue in India and the Wachau Forum in Austria. Our geography defines our mission: Italy is both a continental and Mediterranean nation, with its head in Central Europe, its feet dipped in the Mare Nostrum, and its historical gaze turned toward the Balkans and Eastern Europe. This is a strategic choice for us. We aim to become the central hub—for Africa, which secures development and jobs, and for Europe, which can finally end its dependence on Russia and avoid the nightmare of future energy crises. But it's also a crucial diplomatic choice, one that reestablishes Europe and Africa as natural partners, pushing back against the many destabilizing forces gaining ground in the region.

At first glance, it's not as though African countries are necessarily much more reliable than Russia.

I disagree. Many African nations distrust the West—for reasons we've already discussed—and they're not altogether wrong. Of course, there are and will continue to be unstable countries or governments led by individuals who show little interest in their people's development. Just as there are, and will be, systems that are far from democratic. But that's precisely why we need to pursue strategic investments—because if it's true that democracy fosters development, the opposite is also true: development brings democracy closer. And I can assure you that many countries are making enormous efforts and are simply asking for a stronger presence and more support from us. After all, if the paths to the East are closed—and will likely remain so for some time—the only viable alternative is to open new paths to the South. This strategy also happens to be the most durable tool we have to combat mass illegal immigration, and to guarantee the "right not to have to emigrate," as emphasized by John Paul II and Benedict XVI, and recently recalled by Pope Francis.

This question is twofold: with what money will all this be done, and why should Europe allow you—Italy—to take on such a strategic role?

So, when it comes to funding, a common European effort is clearly needed—both for the investments required in Italy and for those needed along the coast and in African nations. As for why Europe should allow Italy to take on such a strategic role, the answer is simple: because there is no alternative. With Russian energy supplies being turned off, securing new sources is essential. The issue of energy supply must be resolved. Of course, it will require lots of patience and, once again, a great deal of work. It may take at least a decade to begin seeing tangible results—a time frame that may sound long, but in the grand scheme of history, it's not. But let's take it one step at a time: for now, the key is to convince our European partners that we must change course in our strategy toward Africa. In recent years, Europe has withdrawn too much from the continent, leaving the field open to other global players whose interests often don't align with Africa's development, but with its exploitation instead. And in the case where we haven't withdrawn entirely, we've often made serious mistakes.

What are you referring to?

Major strategic errors have been made in Africa. I think of Barack Obama's Nobel Peace Prize–winning foreign policy, which was based on "trust" and support for the so-called "Arab Spring"—a movement that ultimately turned into a long fall and winter of instability. Or the French-led intervention in Libya, strongly backed by the then–President of Italy Giorgio Napolitano and the entire Italian Left, which sought to topple Gaddafi. That decision needs little commentary. More than a decade later, the results speak for themselves.

And what if you don't succeed in this goal that's taking up so much of your time? Aren't you afraid of dedicating a lot of work only to end up with nothing?

Great achievements require time, focus, and sangfroid—as Edmond Dantès, better known as the Count of Monte Cristo, teaches us.

But The Count of Monte Cristo *is a story about revenge. Are you seeking revenge?*

The Count of Monte Cristo is a story about the importance of not letting anyone take from you what is rightfully yours—and about fighting to get it back if it's been unjustly taken. It's a profoundly educational novel.

The Courage to Carry Out Reforms

A Fair, Efficient, Authoritative State

The cabinet meeting ended just a few minutes ago. She meets her staff to finalize the official statement, even though the journalists who have been waiting outside for a couple of hours already know everything—and more. The news agencies are already disseminating the details, reaffirming the rule that nothing is more volatile than political secrets. "Thanks, I'll have a Diet Coke," says the Prime Minister to a staff member who asks if she wants anything, while the building quickly empties of ministers and their entourage of assistants and advisers. In a corner of the room, a small set—two lamps and a video camera—is already set up to record a new episode of *Gli appunti di Giorgia* (Giorgia's Notes), the popular social media video series through which she maintains direct contact with citizens. "Later, later," she tells her team, who are already prepared to start filming. She takes a brief moment to unwind—making a couple of personal phone calls to check that everything is fine at home and to announce yet another delay, quickly scanning major news websites and press agencies to see how the newly approved measures are being received. And then, it's back to us.

Prime Minister, do you really want to change the Constitution?

Yes, and I don't understand why this is causing so much debate. Let me give you a piece of information: from 1948 to today, there have been forty-four constitutional laws, and most of them have amended our Constitution with the approval of practically the entire political spectrum. The first time was in 1958, to adjust the expiration of a transitional provision, and the most recent was in 2022, under the Draghi government, to include the principle of the peculiarity of the islands. In fact, Parliament has attempted this at least two more times—under the Berlusconi government in 2005 and the Renzi government in 2016—but since those reforms did not obtain the qualified majority in Parliament, they were put to a referendum, and the Italian people rejected them. So, I don't understand why the idea of this Parliament making amendments is so scandalous. I've sworn an oath to the Constitution twice, the second time as Prime Minister. Why shouldn't a Center-Right majority have the same prerogatives as others? Especially when, unlike in the past, it has received a clear mandate from the voters to do so?

Because you're aiming high, to change the rules concerning who leads the country, be it the President or the Prime Minister.

As a matter of fact, I'm aiming much higher. My goal is to make this nation governable in an efficient way because I feel the responsibility of leaving Italy in better shape than I found it. I hear people saying that constitutional reform is not a priority right now because we currently have a stable government. But precisely because I have the advantage of favorable conditions that others didn't, it would be irresponsible not to use them to improve the system. I need to consider what will happen afterward, even when we're gone.

You're suggesting a semi-presidential system like France's, in other words, the direct election of the head of state.

That's not completely accurate—the French system is one possible solution, but it's not the only one. We're open to discussing other models with the opposition, such as the premiership, meaning the direct election of the Prime Minister. We're not starting from a predefined model or from the idea that we must simply import one from abroad. There are many models to consider—in fact, I would like to create a new one, an Italian model, one that other nations might even look to in the future. After all, aren't we the birthplace of the law? Our objectives are our starting point, and there are two fundamental goals we want to achieve: government stability and ensuring that Italians have the power to choose who governs the nation. Securing these two pillars means putting an end to governments that change every year and a half, that rise and fall over the heads—and at the expense—of the citizens. It means closing the chapter on political scheming, backroom deals, shifting alliances, and all the tactics that fuel voter disillusionment with politics. Objectives like these should be shared by everyone—or at least by anyone who truly cares about strengthening our democracy. After that, we can work together to determine the best model to achieve them. That's exactly what I proposed when I had talks with the opposition. But the response was somewhat contradictory: on the one hand, there was agreement on the goals; on the other, there was strong resistance to amending the Constitution. The problem is, you can't have both together.

Stability is an obsession of yours.

It's not an obsession, or an ideological fixation. It's realism. The constitutional reform is, with the data at hand, the most important economic reform that can be implemented for Italy.

What does the economy have to do with it?

Let me give you some numbers. In the first nineteen years of the third millennium, Germany had three chancellors, France had four elected presidents, and Italy had fourteen different governments. During the same period, France and Germany saw their GDP grow by more than 20 percent, while Italy's growth was less than 4 percent. Now, either we say that all Italian politicians are less capable than their French and German counterparts—which I don't believe—or we have to face the fact that something in our institutional system isn't working.

What?

The fact is that governments in Italy have an average lifespan of about a year and a half. Does this impact their policies? Let me tell you—it absolutely does. If I know that in one or two years I will be judged on my work, then I'll tend to focus on measures that guarantee immediate public approval. But those measures are often not the most useful ones to apply. This is why, over the years, Italy has consistently prioritized current spending over investment, even though everyone knows that investment spending generates a much higher multiplier effect on economic growth than current spending. The problem with investments is that it takes a few years to see their full benefits, whereas current spending delivers short-term electoral gains. But this is also why Italy has often lacked a strategic vision on major issues. It has not had a clear industrial strategy, it has failed to set long-term priorities, and it has never truly defined its role in the global context. All of this is the result of a political system that has given up on thinking big and looking far ahead.

But our biggest problem is bureaucracy.

That's right, but the two things are connected. Why has bureaucracy become so dominant in Italy? Because politics has been fragile and unstable for years. High-ranking public officials see politicians as temporary figures—and rightly so—because while they remain firmly in place, they have watched dozens of governments come and go. Over time, real power has ended up in their hands. In a way, it's fortunate that Italy has been able to rely on the machinery of the state and its bureaucracy, which has provided a certain degree of stability despite everything. But in the eyes of the public, it is the elected politician who is responsible for the choices made, for what gets done and what doesn't—not the state apparatus. The bureaucracy can ensure continuity, yes, but it cannot do the job that only politics can: having a vision and making decisions. The relationship has been completely reversed, but the fault doesn't lie with the bureaucracy—it lies with politics. Just as it is political weakness that has allowed major economic powers in Italy to do as they please, pursuing their own interests at the expense of the country, without anyone intervening. The scandalous mismanagement of public highway and airport concessions is the saddest example of this.

A rather harsh judgment.

It's not a judgment—it's simply the facts, unfortunately. Take the case of the Fiat group, once perhaps the most recognizable of Italy's major industries. It first became FCA through a merger with Chrysler, and then Stellantis through a merger with the Peugeot group. In 2014, the Agnelli and Elkann families decided to move their legal and tax headquarters abroad, to the Netherlands and the United Kingdom. Of course, they had every right to do so, and they likely gained tax and organizational advantages from it. But the question I ask myself—and I ask you—is: Why didn't German companies like BMW and Volkswagen do the same? Are their executives more naive than those of the former Fiat? They, too, could have gained significant business advantages by relocating. I believe the German state, thanks to stable and authoritative governments, was able to engage more effectively with its major companies, balancing national interests with the need to maintain a competitive industrial sector. Looking beyond Italy, this is exactly what Trump did when some American car manufacturers announced plans to build vehicles in Mexico for the US market. Without hesitation, Trump declared that if those cars were produced in Mexico, they wouldn't be considered American and would be subject to import tariffs in the US. As a result, Ford, for example, had to rethink its plans. Does anything about this case seem different from what happened with Fiat, now Stellantis? I believe the state must go back to acting as a state, restoring the right balance between the public interest and the legitimate private interests of large economic and financial entities. Returning to the example of the automotive industry, I think it's right to support those who manufacture in Italy, create jobs in Italy, and contribute to Italy's industrial ecosystem. This is the approach we are now taking in our discussions with Stellantis. Let me give you another example. It took the horrifying collapse of the Morandi Bridge in Genoa and the tragic death of forty-three innocent people to finally shine a light on disgraceful highway concessions. Billions upon billions were handed to concessionaires without them having to invest a single euro of their own, with clauses preventing the revocation of their contracts—even in cases of serious breaches. And the airport concessions are even worse. A weak political system allowed private groups to rake in billions in profits without taking on business risks, without making their own investments, and without guaranteeing user safety. After the collapse of the Morandi Bridge, the previous government "punished" the Benetton family by giving them around eight billion euros—on top of freeing them from over ten billion in liabilities. A twenty-billion-euro deal. And once again, the major media outlets—generously sponsored by these very groups—made sure not to tell Italians the full story. In short, every major player in the economic landscape feels entitled to pursue only its own interests, without any accountability for the fact that their success is also a product of the support they've received from Italy—beyond just their skill as entrepreneurs—simply because weak institutions, focused only on short-term issues, allow it. In this regard, even the First Republic was better.

It's strange to hear you say that.

Well, no actually. In its own way, the First Republic had a certain stability. Governments changed frequently, but the majority that supported them remained more or less the same. This meant that there was a clear direction—whether right or wrong—that outlasted individual Prime Ministers and ministers. And it's no coincidence that during the hegemony of the Christian Democrats, Italy enjoyed its economic boom. There was continuity, underlying stability, and a long-term strategy. With the Second Republic, however, it has been a constant cycle of starting over again from scratch—an absolute gold mine for business opportunists. And as a result, nothing good has been built.

If things stand as you say they do, why is there such hostility on the Left when the words "constitutional reform" are even uttered?

Because they reason primarily based on the grounds of party interests. And vested party interests tell them two things: the first is that a system in which power is returned to the citizens and taken away from the "palace," which has the power to make and unmake governments, is not advantageous. After all, they are much better at maneuvering within the palace than among the people; the second is that such a system would make impossible the attempts at overturning, the tricks, the toppling of governments carried out by their power system, using tools that have little to do with politics. It is the only possible explanation because there is no other. A reform like this is not beneficial to me or to Brothers of Italy; it benefits the country and all its political class because I assume we might not always win. So, it would also benefit them should they win at the polls. This is why I feel calm when I say that the reform will happen, with or without their support. Because I know that even if they oppose it, it is something done in the interest of Italy, and one day it could even be useful to my opponents. It is a just reform, that is the point. Or at least, that is what I will ask the citizens to confirm when—in the event there are not enough votes to approve it with a two-thirds majority in Parliament—they will be called to express themselves in the confirmatory referendum.

And would the Italians understand? Not to draw comparisons, but with Renzi they didn't understand it.

Renzi's reform didn't touch on this issue, the most important one, and was very messy on the rest. It was convoluted and essentially useless. And then Renzi made the mistake of turning the referendum on the reform into a sort of judgment on his actions and those of his government. A naive choice, which even led a portion of his party—by which, as is well known, Renzi was not particularly liked—to boycott it. I do not believe that the referendum on the constitutional reform should be a referendum on the work of the government or the Prime Minister. I will limit myself to explaining to the citizens how the future of the country can improve, and the Italians will decide what's best for them, independent of me. They gave me the mandate to propose it, with the general elections, and I will propose it. And at that point, they will decide if it should be done. I am only a tool to carry out what they have told me to do. That's why Renzi's precedent does not scare me. In any case, I will work to find an agreement in Parliament with all or a part of the opposition to not "disturb" the Italians. But if I cannot achieve this goal and a referendum becomes necessary, it will be enough to ask two very simple questions. The first: Do you want to decide who should govern? The second: Do you want the person you choose to govern to have five years to do it? These seem to me like two commonsense questions, and Italians have much more common sense than politics often gives them credit for.

Let's stick to reforms but change the topic: regional autonomy.

The Left accuses us of wanting to divide the nation. This, of course, is not true. Imagine if a party like mine, Brothers of Italy, which has made national unity its banner, so much so that it is ironically labeled a neo-Risorgimento movement, could ever aim to divide Italy. Do you think I could claim, I who based the party's name on the words of the national anthem, something that contradicts my own founding principles? Let's not joke around; national unity is not in question, but that doesn't mean that all of Italy's regions have the same problems, needs, and ambitions. On the contrary, stifling legitimate aspirations, and the motivation to give more and do better, can cause exactly the opposite effect, that is, give disorganized voice to dangerously separatist demands. After all, the citizens of Lombardy and Veneto have been waiting for an answer since 2017, when they overwhelmingly approved a referendum that asked for more autonomy. Just as the same desire has been expressed in recent years, in other forms, by other regions such as Emilia-Romagna, Piedmont, Liguria, Tuscany, Umbria, Marche, and Campania. Do we really think that continuing to pretend that nothing is happening is the most productive thing, even for the attachment to the nation of the citizens of those regions? The state must be perceived as a value, not as a cage. That's why I'm convinced that a response must be given. That's why we wrote it in the manifesto, and among its first actions, the government approved the framework bill on autonomy to unlock the process and establish the "rules of the game." We will be consistent with the mandate given to us by the Italians.

Your opponents argue that you are endorsing, for the sake of political opportunism, Matteo Salvini of the League, who has invested a lot in autonomy, especially in the north.

I'm supported by a coalition, and it is my duty to respect the point of view and the demands of the parties that are a part of it. But I still would not have accepted to do something incompatible with my ideas just to secure the government of the nation. The battle for autonomy belongs as much to the League as it does to Brothers of Italy. Autonomy is in the shared political program of the entire Center-Right, which was voted on by the Italians on September 25, 2022. Let me quote it, so that maybe it will be clearer to those who criticize without doing research: "Implement the already initiated path for the recognition of Autonomies under Article 116, paragraph 3 of the Constitution, ensuring all the mechanisms of equality provided for by Article 119 of the Constitution." The point is that I believe that greater autonomy for the regions, built in a certain way and in a certain context, can only be an added value.

In what way and in what context?

As far as the context is concerned, we've already discussed it. Stronger regions are the right counterbalance for a state that must be strong and authoritative. This is why constitutional reform and autonomy, even though they have different paths, are linked together for us. As for the method, the issue is very complex, but I'll try to simplify. The prerequisite for the introduction of differentiated autonomy is the identification of standard parameters that must be guaranteed for everyone. That is, what is the minimum level of services—education, healthcare, transportation, assistance, and so on—that a citizen, regardless of where they live, is entitled to, and therefore what are the resources the state must guarantee to ensure them. The so-called essential levels of services (LEPs). The identification of the LEPs has been discussed for years, but no government has ever managed to define them. We intend to do it because establishing the LEPs represents the best guarantee of cohesion and unity. Once you establish these levels, it's clear that what the virtuous regions—that is, those that are better at managing their responsibilities—do by requesting more powers does not subtract anything from others. That is, the principle of differentiated autonomy is not—as some mistakenly or instrumentally claim—to take from one to give to another. The principle of autonomy is as follows: provided that everyone must have defined parameters of services and rights, regions that demonstrate they are better at guaranteeing them can receive other areas to manage from the state. But this is a matter of the relationship between the state and that region, which does not take anything away from the others. To me, this seems like an opportunity both practically and politically because such a reform necessarily involves holding those who govern the regions more accountable. And it doesn't surprise me that it is precisely those regional presidents, who have had the worst results in government, who are opposing it. These are the same people who accuse the government of "splitting" Italy, talk about cohesion and investment, but then, over the years, have failed to spend billions and billions of euros in European funds.

Reform of the Constitution, reform of the autonomies. The third leg, so to speak, is missing: reform of justice.

It won't be missing, I guarantee it. As you've seen, we've already started. Also because, like the first two, this is a reform that has to do with the economy. Politics often debates—and rightly so—criminal justice because it impacts personal freedom, but the slowness and inefficiency of civil justice can, according to various studies, cost us up to one percentage point of GDP, if not more. It's no coincidence that reducing backlogs and the duration of trials are two of the main objectives of the PNRR [National Recovery and Resilience Plan]: the malfunctioning of the judicial system is potentially capable of canceling its economic stimulus effects.

So this is an obsession of yours.

It's been said many times: the malfunctioning of the justice system, combined with the slowness of the bureaucracy, discourages foreign investors, but above all, it makes our companies less competitive on the international stage. And this is not only true for foreign investments and Italian businesses. In Italy, we also have banks full of Italians' savings, yet a citizen thinks twice before buying a house as an investment, that is, a house to rent out for income because the widespread perception is that if the house were occupied or the tenant defaulted on payments, the justice system would not strongly or quickly defend private property. And this is certainly negative for the individual, but it is also negative for the economic system as a whole.

Do you have any idea why this happens?

In the example I gave you, maybe it's because part of the judiciary, due to its cultural background, is not particularly sensitive to the issue of private property, which it considers, in many cases, a kind of luxury that, as such, doesn't need particular protection. During this conversation, you mentioned an intercepted phone call in which a magistrate says something to the effect of: "We don't apply the law, we stand with the weak." Well, I too stand with the weak, but that doesn't mean I think I can step on the feet of the less weak person, if they are an honest one, because the laws, in a state governed by the rule of law, should apply to them as well. And a citizen who, for example, has worked their whole life and scrimped and saved little by little, which they decide to invest to secure a more peaceful old age, I don't consider strong. And then there's something that really makes me feel upset and that I don't accept.

What's that?

Those politically correct people call them "judicial errors," that is, miscarriages of justice. I would be more direct: "judicial abuses," or, if you prefer, "judicial incompetence." Often, they involve political figures—and that alone is an anomaly—or other well-known individuals. But, in the general silence, most of the time, the victims are ordinary people whose lives are unjustly and violently taken, even if they remain biologically alive. I have read and heard dozens of these stories. How is it possible that this happens? But, more importantly, how is it possible that no one is held personally accountable, as happens when someone makes a serious mistake in any other profession? I am trying to introduce the concept of merit, and responsibility for one's actions is the other side of the same coin. What I mean is: why do judges advance in their careers and receive automatic pay rises, except in rare exceptional cases, simply based on seniority, regardless of how they have worked, the results they have achieved, or the mistakes they have made? For me, it's a mystery, and I think we should address it.

Your predecessors who tried did not have a happy ending.

As you know, Alessandro, I can't be blackmailed, so I'm not afraid. But I will say it clearly: I have no intention of declaring war on the judiciary, which is one of the pillars of democracy. I want to declare war on injustice, not on justice. My conscience and my role demand it. And I'm sure that I have the overwhelming majority of Italian judges on my side in this battle, who are often the first victims of those power dynamics that have placed affiliation above merit.

I don't doubt it, but that is a caste with very strong bonds inside all the institutions.

You yourself described the famous "system" when you interviewed the now former judge and former president of the National Magistrates' Association, Luca Palamara. But I have come this far precisely to change the various systems that have proven to be ineffective or even, as in the case we are discussing, to be like a virus within democracy.

Right, but where do we start from?

Let's do it this way because it's simpler: I will tell you where I want it to finish.

Go ahead.

Among the many, there is a case of miscarried justice that particularly struck me, I would say tormented me. Your colleague Giulio Golia told the story on *Le Iene*, the satirical TV show about politics. The story was about a man named Saverio who was sentenced for the most wretched of crimes: sexual violence against his two children. Although he proclaimed his innocence, he was convicted and went to jail. After a legal battle lasting more than fifteen years, the case was reopened, and it was discovered that none of it was true. The sentence was quashed, and he was released. But by that time, his life was in tatters. Well, I want to make sure that this kind of thing will never happen again. What method will I use? Simply the most authentically liberal one: more guarantees for the accused and defendants in the exercise of their sacred right to defense, without depriving the judiciary of important investigative tools to ascertain crimes. And more justice for those given a definitive sentence. In other words, I will give you the maximum guarantee during the trial phase, but once you are convicted, you will serve the sentence.

The latest report from the Ministry of Justice says: in one year, 562 citizens received compensation for wrongful detention, which cost us €24.5 million. For these errors, the Ministry of Justice has proposed fifty disciplinary actions over the course of three years, none of which resulted in sanctions (nine acquittals, fourteen cases dismissed, and twenty-seven ongoing).

It seems clear to me that we are not in a good place. So, this is what I say: instead of presenting any attempt at reform as a clash between politics and the judiciary, instead of pontificating about the independence and autonomy of judges, do we want to talk about this, in substance, or not? Do we want to make it increasingly difficult for an innocent person to face the ordeal that Saverio did, that is, an innocent person ending up in prison? Shall we try to make sure that large companies no longer prefer to invest elsewhere, also because they are afraid of the slowness and delays of the Italian justice system?

I have to insist: What's the recipe?

We have the slowest justice system in Europe. We have an excessively high rate of cases, compared to the average, that end up in nothing. There is an excessive use of preventive detention. There is, as you just mentioned, a troubling number of judicial errors recognized by the judiciary itself, yet not sanctioned. We have a problem with the media protection of citizens involved, directly or indirectly, in investigations even before the trial begins, or who are exposed to public ridicule even though they are not involved in anything. Since we have all these problems, and we all know it, the government has already started to respond with the first part of the justice reform. A reform in a decidedly more liberal direction, countering the media spectacle of trials, intervening to protect citizens' privacy in the context of wiretapping, offering more guarantees to Italians during the precautionary measures phase, without depriving the judiciary of investigative tools. Then, we will focus on the slowness of civil justice: more streamlined procedures, greater use of digitization, hiring, and streamlining the selection process for judges. Civil justice must become a driver again, not a burden for the Italian economy. But we can't hide behind the curtain: the best reforms must still be carried out by people. So, to answer your question, I think that, together and not against the judges, we must sit at a table and, beyond the legislative interventions, solve the issue at its root: without a reform of the *Consiglio Superiore della Magistratura* [CSM, or High Council of the Judiciary], freeing it once and for all from the shackles of politicized currents, which then simply translates into the exchange of favors, we can forget about resolving it in a structural and definitive way. Moreover, I would like to start a small but significant cultural revolution: to make all public employees, whatever position they hold and wherever they are assigned, rediscover the awareness, now somewhat lost, that the work they do is a service to the state. They are civil servants and they must feel proud of what their role is. They need to be aware that their work determines the future of people, families, and businesses. That going to work has meaning and purpose. And this, within the judiciary system, is perhaps very clear. Because the speed of a trial does not only depend on the judge but also on the clerk handling that case. I dream of an Italy where everyone does their bit with the utmost commitment.

They won't let you reform the CSM; they're stronger than you.

First of all, I would like there not to be a "we" and a "they," because we and they should all be together, the state. Then, let me remind you that just five years ago, everyone was stronger than Brothers of Italy. In the 2018 elections, we got 4 percent, and today we're at around 30 percent. And yet, we are the same, we are the same thing. If I am convinced of an argument, as I think I've already said, I'm not afraid to start from a position of lesser strength. What's that saying? Oh, yes: time will tell.

Of course, only time will tell, but time also runs out in some areas. For example, financial markets have very tight deadlines to make their decisions, and the European Union also sets a time limit within which Italy's accounts must be balanced. How much time is Giorgia Meloni giving herself to meet these deadlines?

All Things Considered

Decline Is Not a Destiny

The Prime Minister addresses me with a firm voice: "I'm going to be clear, me and you are not going to get along this way." To which I reply with concern: "What do you mean by that, Prime Minister?" First, she swallows something she was chewing on, and then she explains: "During this conversation, I have eaten"—she raises two fingers—"first, a piece of bittersweet chocolate, and just now, another piece of chocolate, this one white, which, among other things, tasted like soap. It's your fault that my diet has gone to pot." I draw a sigh of relief and ask: "Are you saying you're on a diet?" She answers: "No I'm not, but I ought to be. Every morning, I go on a diet, which I generally quit around lunchtime. Today, I had managed to stay on my diet until the evening, then I started talking to you, and once again I'm going to have to start over again tomorrow." She tells me that before becoming Prime Minister she would do physical exercise at least four times a week. "Between the training that there's absolutely no way I can do now, the sandwiches I'm forced to have for lunch, and dinner almost always around midnight, I've become like a sack of potatoes. But now I'm going to take the proper measurements—not those of my waistline, I'm not brave enough, the figurative ones of the government activity—and then I promise you I'm going to get myself back on track. Also because if I keep this up, I'll have to start wearing my maternity clothes again." Fine then, let's continue, or rather, let's rewind the tape for this evening.

Prime Minister, when you took over the country was €2,762 billion in the red, equal to 145 percent of the gross domestic product, better known by the acronym GDP. The kind of thing that keeps you up at night.

I'm in the same situation that Mario Draghi and a dozen of my predecessors all found themselves in. But on this matter, I will be particularly alert, for many reasons, but for one especially.

Which one?

The most obvious of the economic laws: the amount of debt intersects with the extent of your freedom.

Good, so how free are we?

Not enough to be able not to be careful, that is, behave as if there were no tomorrow. Much more than can be imagined by reading the figures I have just quoted, because the debt in actual fact tells us a lot but not everything.

What doesn't it say?

It does not say, for example, that Italy—even though it may seem paradoxical at first sight—has its finances in order, and, setting aside the two years of the pandemic, has long been running a primary surplus, meaning that, net of interest payments on the debt, the state collects more money than it spends. In this respect, we have been among the most virtuous for years, despite the waste that we unfortunately allowed ourselves in the past. To be more precise, according to the data of the International Monetary Fund [IMF], we rank eleventh in the global list of the least spendthrift countries, better, for example, than France, Germany, Spain, and the United Kingdom. If we were a family, we would say: it's not that we're squandering money; it's just that at the end of the month, we have a mortgage that we really can't afford, and that ultimately takes a significant portion of our salary.

The infamous interest on the debt, that is, on the government bonds with which we financed ourselves, evidently not always for the right reasons.

That's right, but I don't think this is the place to talk about a past for which I bear no responsibility. We're trying to think about the future here, and I also believe that the future is not preordained or inevitable, even as concerns such a complicated matter.

So how do we change this future?

First of all, my goal is to be able to deal with the things I consider necessary for this country with greater freedom, without having to be so constrained by the perception these choices generate abroad, in the markets. But I fully understand that, naturally, this cannot ignore the importance given to debt. The solution would be obvious: let's cut the debt. Right, but as I said before, in day-to-day affairs, we're virtuous. Today, the state doesn't throw away billions on useless things, even though—allow me to say this only because we're trying to fix it—with universal income, the 110 percent Superbonus for building renovations, school desks with wheels, and bonuses for scooters; those who came before me really made some ridiculous blunders. Can we spend less? Not much less. If anything, we can spend better, and we're trying to do just that. But can we, for example, further cut social spending? No, we can't, nor is it my intention to do so. So then what?

Right, so then what?

The primary goal is not just to make cuts, though wherever there is waste, of course; cuts are welcome, nor solely to spend better, because that's not enough. The only truly useful thing that can be done in this regard is to fuel growth. Common sense tells us this, but so does history. All you have to do is remember the Monti government in 2011: in a particularly acute crisis situation, Monti intervened drastically in all areas, applying that much-celebrated austerity advocated by Europe. The result? That recipe left us with an anemic economy. I am not a Nobel Prize for Economics winner, but I think in the opposite way: debt stability can only be guaranteed with sustained growth, driven by investments, not with savage cuts that further depress the economy. If you weaken growth to guarantee debt stability, you're actually putting that very stability at risk.

To this regard, allow me to remind you of Margaret Thatcher's speech, in 1988, to the College of Europe in Bruges, which is often referred to as the Bruges Speech, or the speech of the three "nos." The Iron Lady didn't agree with what her European colleagues were doing, and, to sum up the concepts of her speech, she set several principles:

> *Britain does not dream of some cozy, isolated existence on the fringes of the European Community. Our destiny is in Europe, as part of the Community. That is not to say that our future lies only in Europe, but nor does that of France or Spain or, indeed, of any other member. The Community is not an end in itself. Nor is it an institutional device to be constantly modified according to the dictates of some abstract intellectual concept. Nor must it be ossified by endless regulation. The European Community is a practical means by which Europe can ensure the future prosperity and security of its people in a world in which there are many other powerful nations and groups of nations. We Europeans cannot afford to waste our energies on internal disputes or arcane institutional debates. They are no substitute for effective action. Europe has to be ready both to contribute in full measure to its own security and to compete commercially and industrially in a world in which success goes to the countries which encourage individual initiative and enterprise, rather than those which attempt to diminish them.*

Margaret Thatcher was the leader of the Conservative Party, and not just the British one, right? Today I am the president of the ECR Party, the European Party of Conservatives and Reformists, and I agree with her speech wholeheartedly. Even though you have to start from the premise that the United Kingdom and Continental Europe have very different histories as concerns the process of European integration. The UK joined the EEC [European Economic Community] much later than we did, after a troubled path, and they left the EU following the end of a very difficult domestic debate. In Great Britain, the European spirit has always coexisted with that of an island open to the rest of the world, fearful of being limited in its global inclinations by the rules imposed by Brussels. With Brexit, the latter prevailed, empowered by a currency like the pound sterling, the financial hub of London, and an economic, political, and commercial context like the Commonwealth. That is not the case for Italy, whose inclination can only be European. So, let's clear the field of any hypotheses of Italy exiting the EU, to avoid any misunderstandings. However, that does not mean we should not have the courage to reflect on what has worked and what has not among the European rules.

Let's talk in more practical terms.

So, if we continue to think in terms of the Fiscal Compact . . .

Let me interrupt you to help the readers: the Fiscal Compact is the agreement signed in 2012 by all the European States—except, not by accident, the United Kingdom—that commits each country to keep its national public debt within certain limits agreed upon with Brussels.

That's it exactly. I was saying that if you have to cut public spending every year to stay within those strict parameters, as things stand, we're in trouble, because over the past ten years we have already cut a lot, in some cases even too much, and it's hard to go further. One thing we're trying to do, for example, is to convince the European Union not to revert to imposing the strict budget constraints that existed before the pandemic, which, as is well known, were suspended to allow States to cope with the COVID pandemic and the economic damage it wreaked. And, thank God, there is now practically unanimous agreement on the need to reform the Stability and Growth Pact. The point now is how to reform it. If we had to put it in a few words, after years in which the pact's rules served almost exclusively for stability, now the time has come for them to be primarily geared toward growth, if only for the sake of fairness. The big challenge, from our perspective, is to separate investment spending—particularly in the sectors that Europe has defined as strategic, namely green and digital transition, but also defense—from the calculation of the deficit-to-GDP ratio. Even before Mario Draghi made it famous, we supported the idea of distinguishing between *good* debt and *bad* debt. We would not consider it fair or useful to have a new Stability Pact that brings together current spending and investment spending within the same category. The former has no effect on growth, while the latter produces growth, contributes to wealth creation, and thus helps reduce debt, just as a company does not list utility bills and expenses for purchasing new machinery under the same budget line. Keeping current spending under control is essential, but investment spending should enjoy greater freedom or at least more flexibility; otherwise, the country grinds to a halt. Moreover, those who invest in Italy, that is, those who buy our government bonds, don't just look at the debt: the figure they are most interested in and willing to bet on is growth. How does the stock market think? If a company is growing, it is attractive, regardless of its debt; if it's not growing, then before buying, one looks first at how much debt it has.

Allow me to simplify: to grow, you need investments, and to invest, you need money. Well, Europe—partly through grants and partly through loans at very low interest rates—gave us a huge amount of it with the by now famous PNRR, which stands for the National Recovery and Resilience Plan: over 200 billion euros. So, problem solved, right?

I get the irony of this, but I do consider it as such. And here we go back to the main point: if you give me money to promote growth through investments and then punish me with budget rules because I make those investments, that makes very little sense. That said, the PNRR is a great opportunity, but like every great opportunity, it requires all of us to move in the same direction. I didn't write that plan, and I didn't even vote for it because when it was brought to Parliament, we were asked to vote on it blindly, without even reading it, and I'm too serious a person to take on a responsibility of that kind. But I know it well, and it needs some tweaking, as well as a great commitment from everyone to spend the resources on time and in the best possible way. Instead, here in Italy, a strategic issue like the PNRR is being exploited to attack the government. Every day, someone stirs up a media brawl on the topic, launching unfounded and false accusations, not based on data or knowledge of the rules, hoping that this will make the markets nervous, that this nervousness could turn into a storm, and that the storm will eventually bring down the government. Anti-Italian sentiment, but this too is something new. Once I read a great story by Umberto Eco, one of our most world-famous intellectuals. In Eco's words:

> Some years ago in New York I found myself having a conversation with a taxi driver whose name I had difficulty in placing. He was, he explained, Pakistani and asked where I came from. Italy, I replied. He asked how many of us there were and was surprised we were so few and that our language wasn't English. Then he asked me who our enemies were. In response to my "Sorry?" he explained patiently that he wanted to know who were the people against whom we had fought through the centuries over land claims, ethnic rivalry, border incursions, and so forth. I told him we are not at war with anyone. He explained that he wanted to know who were our historical enemies, those who kill us and whom we kill. I repeated that we don't have any, that we fought our last war more than half a century ago—starting, moreover, with one enemy and ending with another. He wasn't satisfied. How can a country have no enemies? Getting out of the taxi, I left a two-dollar tip to compensate him for our indolent Italian pacifism. And only then did it occur to me how I should have answered. It is not true that we Italians have no enemies. We have no outside enemies, or rather we are unable to agree on who they are, because we are continually at war with each other.[2]

I think that there is some truth in this paradox.

It is obvious that we, as the Italian system, have difficulties in implementing the PNRR projects within the expected time frames, as

---

2 Eco, Umberto. *Inventing the Enemy: Essays*. Houghton Mifflin Harcourt, 2012, pp. 2–3.

unfortunately has always happened with European funds, because we are a brilliant and capable people, but also good at complicating our own lives sometimes. However, the rigidity of the PNRR and the short implementation times should also be considered a challenge to be overcome together, an opportunity to modernize our system. To paraphrase Francesco Guccini, not exactly a fan of mine, and his beautiful song about Christopher Columbus, destiny challenges us to push ourselves to be proud of who we are. In this game, we should act as one: majority and opposition, journalists and magistrates, intellectuals and ordinary people, because what is at stake here is not the government, but the modernization of Italy and its credibility in the eyes of the world. And yet, no, some are rooting for failure, as if that money would end up in my pocket, my party's pocket, or only my voters' pockets. Let me give you an example. During the long negotiations with the European Commission for the payment of the third installment—in fact, objectives that were the responsibility of the previous government—I was shocked by a letter that the CGIL [Italian General Confederation of Labor, a national trade union] and its students, the UDU [Union of University Students], sent to Ursula von der Leyen, asking her to verify the achievement of the target on student housing because, according to them, the target had not been met. Can you believe it? Italians who write to Europe to ask that it not give any money to Italy. Italians who hate Italians, especially in politics. But you know what? I love all of Italy, I do what's in its interests and I don't hate anyone. So we will get that money on the ground, come what may. We'll tweak the bits that don't work well, prioritizing projects with a strategic profile, negotiating with the European Commission on everything necessary, and we'll pass the laws that are needed to overcome the delays and difficulties of bureaucracy and local authorities. We will continue to work to ensure greater synergy between the various sources of European funding, looking at the PNRR with a strategic and comprehensive vision alongside cohesion policies, both to guarantee that the resources are actually spent and to prioritize quality measures capable of having concrete effects on the GDP. We will do what needs to be done, and we will get everyone working together. And if someone wants to stay up in the gallery throwing paper balls at us while we're working below, so be it. When we're done, we will have taught them another lesson. Having said that, I am clearheaded enough to understand the danger of the "eco doctrine."

Let's hear it.

We're talking about debt and growth, right? Good. We refinance our debt by placing government bonds on the market: you lend me the money, and I give it back to you in three, five, or ten years with interest. If there is confidence in the country, it is the safest investment a saver can make. Now, until finance became a global factor, Italian government bonds were mostly bought by Italian citizens who, as a result, grew a little richer and used this wealth for consumption or investments in Italy. And since the savings of our families have always been substantial, the system worked with mutual benefits. For many years, this has no longer been the case, and today a large part of our debt is held, directly or indirectly, by foreign banks and funds. On the one hand, this is certainly a good thing because we can place a larger amount of bonds. But on the other hand, we need to be cautious: we can't rule out that those who buy our bonds abroad—I'm not referring to the individual private investor but to large entities scattered around the world—might decide from one day to the next not to repurchase them, or even to sell them suddenly. This could happen for reasons that might not only be economic but also linked to other issues, causing problems for us.

It has been ascertained that in 2011, the surge of the spread that led to the fall of the Berlusconi government was triggered by the sudden and massive sale of Italian government bonds held by Deutsche Bank, the principal German bank, during a period when Chancellor Angela Merkel did not have the best relations with Silvio Berlusconi.

I have extensively stated, in the past, how, from my point of view, that event unfolded. Here, I will simply point out how it is evident that having too much debt in foreign hands can become a powerful weapon used to interfere in the policies of sovereign states, especially for countries like ours with such a high debt. This is the reason why I was extremely proud of the government's decision to issue government bonds with excellent returns specifically dedicated to small Italian savers. With the single "BTP Valore," in just a few days, we raised over eighteen billion Euros solely from Italian families, a record from every point of view.

I understand, but what is the paradox supposed to be?

Well, the paradox is that you are not just pressured by those who decide to use their own money to buy Italian government bonds, but also by foreign entities that buy part of the Italian debt with the Italians' own money. This is because a significant portion of Italians' savings ends up in banks under foreign control or in foreign investment funds; and these entities, using Italians' money, buy Italian government bonds. At the end of the day, foreign investors impact—to put it mildly—the Italian state thanks to Italians' own money.

A paradox. But I think it's an inevitable scenario.

Maybe in part. But going back to conceiving Italy's entire credit and financial system as a strategic factor for the nation would help limit the damage. And then, we have to make sure that Europe does not create further tensions and problems in the government bond market.

Is that happening?

A sensitive issue concerns the banking system. Under pressure from Germany, there is an attempt to introduce something called "risk weighting" into the European banking system. What does it mean? As is well known, banks purchase large quantities of government bonds from sovereign states as part of their investments, which are listed under "assets." Well, Europe would like to say: since Italian government bonds are considered, due to the debt, riskier than German or French ones, you—whether you're a bank or an insurance company, even an Italian one—can hold fewer of them to avoid jeopardizing your solvency. I've watered it down, but that's essentially the idea. And if such a thing were to pass, we would find ourselves in trouble because our debt would become less sustainable than before—not because of a loss of confidence, not because we'd be on the brink of bankruptcy, but simply because of the change in European rules imposed on banks and insurance companies. I can't accept that. Thatcher's words come to mind.

If that's the case, I'd like to remind you that Ronald Reagan, another icon of the Republicans and conservatives, once said: "The national debt is big enough to take care of itself."

Yes, the idea is that the main task of those who govern is to unleash energy; everything else follows. For this reason, for example, we have significantly simplified the procurement code—those 630 articles of law, I repeat, 630, that, theoretically intended to prevent criminal infiltration and various forms of opacity, ended up strangling the possibility of opening a construction site or completing a contract within the necessary time frames and conditions. This monstrosity has mostly created obstacles to growth, yet when we announced our reform—which, by the way, was planned by the previous government and written with the fundamental contribution of the Court of Public Auditors—the opposition was up in arms: "Meloni, the partner of mafiosi, of the corrupt, of thieves." And the best part is that those who insult you are the same ones who wrote the building bonus measures, with their billions in confirmed fraud against the state. I refuse to take lessons from people like that. We start from a very simple principle: while any law must be defined and circumscribed, the creativity of those who steal has no limits or boundaries. So, no matter how much you, as a legislator, do, there will always be a scoundrel trying to take advantage. The 630 articles of the previous procurement code did not solve the problem of corruption or infiltration; they only suppressed our healthy entrepreneurship, paralyzed administrators with the "fear of signing," and blocked the system. The method must be changed.

In other words?

The approach we adopt for public contracts is the same one we want to apply to every field: on the one hand, simplifying regulations and life as much as possible; on the other, intensifying the checks and sanctions. The idea is simple: the more I make things easier for you, the stricter I must be if you still try to cheat me. We've already said this, I believe, but I insist because it is important: the main path to increasing revenue is not to adopt an aggressive, oppressive stance toward citizens. You have to say: I want you to work because your work benefits me in return. So, if you work, our interests align, and as long as they align, I will walk alongside you. But if you cheat me, our interests are no longer aligned, and I must be relentless—not by adding more regulations, red tape, or hassle, but simply by being more effective at catching you and harsher in enforcing the penalties. And this does not apply just to public contracts.

I suppose you're referring to the taxation, the famous tregua fiscale, *or "tax let-off."*

Exactly, it's part of another fundamental reform that we've been waiting for for half a century: the tax reform, which has just been definitively approved by Parliament. Our enabling law states the same underlying principle: on the one hand, I allow you, if there has been no fraud, to regularize your position as far as possible. And even here, the opposition tears its hair out in despair, accusing us of far-fetched amnesties, of helping cheats and tax evaders, and so on. But they're lying. We simply start from a principle of common sense: if you declared what you owed to the tax authorities, but then didn't pay, it's reasonable to assume your intention wasn't to evade taxes—otherwise, you wouldn't have declared anything. I have to assume that you had difficulty paying, and considering the complicated years since the pandemic, I can't rule that out; or maybe your tax declaration was inaccurate because of all the tax rules. So here's what we'll do: you pay everything you owe, I apply a small late-payment penalty of 3 to 5 percent, but I allow you to pay in installments over the long term. I assume you want to pay and not cheat me, so I'll put you in the position to do so. Then, I'll create a taxpayers' charter that provides you with more protection and will connect all the databases I have. So, if I realize you're trying to cheat me, I'll be much stricter than my predecessors were.

Would you repeat the phrase that caused quite a storm, the one about taxes imposed on store owners that would be a kind of state extortion?

I never said that taxes are a state extortion. I said something very different. For too long, there has been a wrong approach to the collecting taxes that have been evaded. The tax authorities are given the task of achieving a specific overall goal, and this often results in harassing businesses that operate transparently. Because the easiest thing is to go after them for money instead of going after total evaders or sophisticated billion-dollar frauds. We will change this approach. What I want to say is that when you're an honest person and you start to fear the tax authorities, there's something wrong, especially when you find yourself facing a state that turns out to be strong with the weak and weak with the strong.

An international investigation that started in Germany in 2018 uncovered a massive tax fraud in Europe amounting to fifty-five billion euros, involving banks and investment funds. In Italy, the confirmed shortfall was 4.5 billion euros. The case was closed with a settlement around one hundred million euros. Is this what you're referring to?

This and much more. You know, as is to be expected, large financial and industrial groups have the economic power to go through legal battles with teams of top-notch lawyers working full-time. But I'm also referring to injustices that happen in everyday life, at much lower levels. Take a storeowner, for example: electronic invoicing, electronic payments, receipts, accounts ledgers, and everything else we know. But if there's an inspection, you can be sure they'll find something awry, even if it's just a minor issue. It would be flawless if the same rigor were applied to the guy who, just a few feet away, on the same pavement, sells goods spread out on a sheet thrown on the ground; whether what he's selling is counterfeit or the real thing is of no concern. These two individuals, so to speak, are doing the same job in the same country, under the same laws, and even on the same street: you find a flaw in the first and hit them with a penalty, while with the second, you don't even ask for a document, and of course, that person continues to evade taxes without a worry in the world. This cannot continue, and it's what we're working on because it's clear to everyone that there are unregulated zones outside the State's control, and that very same state is then tough on honest people. And that's not all.

Continue.

Take the example of small convenience stores. There are our local, traditional neighborhood stores, and those that open on the initiative of some small entrepreneur trying their luck. Then there are those, which are multiplying like mushrooms in our cities, opened and run by non-EU citizens, mostly of Asian origin. Does the tax office carry out tight checks on the first or the second group? The first group, of course. And the reason is simple: the Italian owner can be traced, he already exists from a fiscal point of view, he doesn't run away, and in any case, we know where he is and what to take from him. The foreigner who opens a convenience store, in most cases, starts out formally according to the law, but after two years, which is the maximum time after which you can no longer claim excuses for not paying taxes, they shut the business and vanish, and in their place, a partner takes over. The cycle continues indefinitely. And the state, which can't figure out how to deal with it, finds a way to recover the missing resources from the Italian business owner mentioned previously. What should we call this? Unfair competition, free-for-all tax dodging?

I can already hear them saying: here comes Meloni blaming immigrants, in this case, the Chinese or the Bangladeshi.

Not at all. I'm saying something different. I'm saying that it's not fair that, since you can't get money from the pop-up shops run by foreigners, you then turn to Italian storekeepers to make up for it. And I remember that we intervened in this area with a measure included in the budget law that today makes it much more difficult to play this open-and-shut game with companies, which every year produces billions of euros in tax evasion. We had proposed it for years when we were the opposition, but, inexplicably, it was always rejected. The same thing goes for rave parties, another measure highly contested by the opposition. All people talked about was the safety aspect of illegal raves, but it's really much more complicated. I remember when we passed the law, there was an interview with a man who complained that he would no longer be able to sell his shish kebabs at rave parties. It drove a friend of mine crazy, who, incidentally, organizes events for a living. At one point, he sent me this message: "It's not that you can't have a rave, of course you can. Open a VAT number, rent or buy the venue, hire a company to handle security and follow all the rules; hire regular staff, get fire extinguishers, pay all the taxes involved, and so on. Get a fiscal cash register connected to the Revenue Agency, get authorization for the sale of food and drinks, cook all the shish kebabs you want, and throw your great party with as many people as the area can legally accommodate. Just like all of us poor idiots do." That's what normal people think. The Left defends raves, defends the rights of fake immigrant entrepreneurs? It doesn't surprise me. In the end, it's always them defending illegality, and that's why no one understands them anymore. Meanwhile, we don't ban raves, or even the free trade of non-EU immigrants; we only ban the attempt to do so illegally, that is, without respecting the laws of the Italian state. And that is the most serious way I know to make people start trusting the state again.

Of course, but it's also illegal for Italians not to pay taxes.

A patriot cannot be a tax dodger; it's a contradiction in terms. Someone with a strong sense of national pride feels part of the national community and feels obliged to contribute to its well-being.

Let's be honest, that's not always the case—or at least it doesn't always happen.

Precisely because I want to be honest, I say that trust is built not only on example but also on clear and well-defined rules for everyone. I warn you that with us, the widespread "friends of friends" model does not apply, and it won't: the idea that I turn a blind eye to you, then go next door and punish someone else. For this reason, too—clarity, simplicity, and responsibility—we have begun the process of a structural tax reform.

The famous "flat tax."

Not just that, but I understand that it's perceived as the big novelty. I would call it an "incentive mechanism": of all that you invoice more than the previous years, you get to keep most of it, so it's in your interest to work more and better. In the short term, in terms of budget sustainability, a flat tax for everyone is not feasible, but we started with three different flat taxes: expanding the flat tax for self-employed workers, the flat tax on income increases compared to the previous year, and the flat tax on productivity bonuses for workers. In short, we're advancing step by step to see how it goes. The next step is this: I would like to see it applied to all wage increases for employees. This is the message: we are in a tough situation, the international situation is what it is, but if you believe in it and roll up your sleeves, I will acknowledge what you've done—give me your best, and you'll be rewarded. And this goes back to merit, the real driving force of any society. Then there's the need to review the issue of income tax brackets, significantly expanding the first and lowest bracket to include as many employees as possible. This has been proven: if you reduce the level of a very high tax, the tax base expands, which means that, despite the generalized reduction in taxes, the state does not lose revenue—actually, it even increases it. The first to do this, in 1985, was Ronald Reagan in a weak and confused America. That move was later called "the Second American Revolution," and it had remarkable effects, especially as concerned the middle class, which is what drives any economy. I'll sum it up: lower taxes, the rule of law, a clear and firm position on the international stage with Italy playing a leading role in Europe and the Mediterranean—these are some of the key points of the revolution I have in mind. But I intend to assess this difficult and complex task when we get to the end of this journey of ours.

I'm Still Giorgia

And I've Said Everything I Have to Say

We've talked a lot about politics. Now let me ask the most political question of all. How are you experiencing all of this, personally, I mean?

It's also the hardest question to answer of all of them. Do you want to know whether I like it? No, I don't like it, and I knew I wasn't going to like it. What I mean to say is that these are months, actually years, when you have to give up everything. As if your life were suspended. Many of the people who find themselves in my same situation offset what they have to give up with the personal satisfaction of being at the heart of the scene. Let's say that I'm particular when it comes to that. It may seem hard to believe, but I don't like all this visibility. When push comes to shove, I'm actually quite shy, and so I find it hard to deal with this. I loathe going around with all these people accompanying me, I loathe the sirens, I can't stand the fact that when you're in my position, whatever you say, write, even a simple remark, a facial expression, can be used against you. I'm scared that this awareness on my part will gradually replace my naturalness, that it will change me, when the goal I have always set for myself is to continue to be the way I am. I've always felt sorry for those politicians who have tried to sell themselves as being something that is very different from what they are. Plus, I'm so jealous of normality and independence, of the simple things that are increasingly becoming a luxury in my everyday life. On paper, I shouldn't drive a car, go food shopping, take my daughter to school, spend time in a gym open to the public, have a drink with my friends before dinner. That's what it says on paper, but these are rules I simply can't abide by. I wouldn't be able to stand it. Besides, preserving your usual lifestyle helps you to work better. This is a period of transition in my life, and I won't allow this experience to change me: I need to be ready to leave my job and go back to my previous life from one minute to another. I will fight for this, too, but it's just another battle to be added to all the others.

Before you became Prime Minister you always refused to have a security detail.

That's right, and I would do the same now if I could. At first, it drove me crazy to think that people with a family would be forced to abandon it if, for instance, on Christmas Eve, I decided to go to Milan to spend the evening with my in-laws. I tried to convince them not to accompany me, but then I realized that for them the suggestion was tantamount to an insult. Because in their eyes I'm not Giorgia, I'm the Prime Minister, the head of the Italian government. An institution that, as such, must be protected, because the honor and authoritativeness of Italy is at stake. My impact with the security detail was one of the most difficult things for me, at first. However, they're all extraordinary men and women, and little by little we have become friends. We started by using nicknames, then we moved on to the clichés, stories, and legends. Now I feel at home with them, and I sincerely hope that they are proud to work with me. Their professionalism is unparalleled, and they are the absolute best at their jobs. But I believe they are also proud of what I do, and that they view their sacrifices in a different way.

In any case, between work, security, lack of freedom and all the rest, this job is a nightmare for you.

Let's not exaggerate. I experience it for what it is and for what it has to be: a responsibility so great that it leaves no room to be selfish. And, in the end, the fact that I won't be unhappy when this experience comes to an end has one essential advantage: I'm not willing to do whatever it takes to remain glued to my seat. I will continue to hold this job for as long as the conditions allow me to do it properly. Should those conditions no longer exist, I would have no problem stepping aside. In any case, this commitment is filled with satisfaction and emotion, along with the affection and encouragement of the many Italians who believe in you. That is what makes it worth it.

All told, you politicians are a privileged group of people.

No doubt we are, especially because we're paid a lot for our work. Even though I, as Prime Minister, am paid just as much as an ordinary Member of Parliament. I only say this because there's all sorts of fake news in the social media.

What was your biggest emotion since becoming Prime Minister?

Two come to mind. The first was the day I took office, when I went before the military guard of honor welcoming me into the courtyard of Palazzo Chigi. I was absolutely shaking. For a person like me who is moved just to hear the Italian national anthem and to see the flag, hearing "honor to the Prime Minister of the Republic of Italy," with the trumpets playing and the troops in formation, made my heart skip a beat. I looked at those men and women in uniform standing to attention one by one, and all I could think of were all the others who risked their lives, who sacrificed their lives for Italy. Deep down I thought, *I will not disappoint you.* Still today, after dozens of military events, I am moved each time, but the first time was unforgettable.

There was the mystery of the shoes that day. When you arrived, you were wearing laced up low-heeled black shoes, but during the ceremony when you exchanged the bell with Mario Draghi you were wearing high heels . . .

Yes, I remember. There's no mystery and not really a lot to say about it, actually. I had put on my heels, but then before leaving the house I worried that I might trip on them during the ceremony. It was an important moment for me, and I didn't want to take that risk. So I wore low heels for the military honors, and then changed into high heels when I got to my office.

You said there were two moments. What was the second one?

It was when I called the mother of Alessia Piperno, the young woman who had been arrested and imprisoned in Iran during the period when people were protesting in the streets against the regime. I had the privilege of telling her that her daughter would be coming home. We started working on her release right from the start, but it was a delicate situation, on the razor's edge. One wrong word could have undermined the results. Alessia's mother had written a beautiful letter pleading with me to help her bring her daughter back home. There was no need to convince me, I was already dealing with it. The morning that the plane carrying Alessia took off from Teheran, and she was finally safe, I called her mother, Manuela. But when she answered, her voice was so fraught with emotion, so filled with both hope and despair, that I started crying, too, and all I could get out were the words "Alessia is coming home." The embrace between mother and daughter, and with the whole family, when she arrived in Ciampino, made me say: "What a wonderful job I have." Something I have rarely found myself saying.

Which has been the worst day since you became Prime Minister?

There have been many difficult days, it's hard to say which of them was the worst. There are days when, all day long, every time the phone rings it's because something has gone wrong. But I've learned to live with it. I'm going to tell you a secret: I've always been a rather pessimistic person, as well as a rather anxious one. I'm very surprised by . . . I wouldn't know how to define it . . . my serenity? No, maybe the concentration with which I am dealing with this phase in my life. I would never have expected it, and it is one of the few things I can't make head or tail of. There have been periods along the way when my responsibilities were definitely fewer than they are today, but for which I was much more anxious than I am now. I don't know what happened. Perhaps, after all, it's like when your legs wobble before an important race, but then, when the race begins, your legs stop wobbling and they know exactly what to do. It's as if my head had decided that anxiety is a pointless waste of energy. This is the only logical answer I've given myself. Of course, I also try to keep as far away from the constant attempts to destabilize things. I'm sure that there are lots of people working to try to make me lose my temper, but so far they haven't succeeded. I hardly read the newspapers, the articles, the comments. I don't normally watch the TV shows that are about me. And not because I don't respect them, or because I don't respect the work of the journalists who produce them, but simply because I don't want to be influenced. My rule is to do what my conscience tells me to do. That is my intention. There have been lots of sad days, too. The terrible flooding in Ischia, in Emilia-Romagna, the Cutro massacre. And the days I lost some of my friends, like Andrea Augello and Silvio Berlusconi.

How did you feel when you heard that Berlusconi had died?

As you can imagine, I was one of the first to know, and the impact was very strong, strange, unexpected. We all knew he wasn't well, we knew that sooner or later that day would come, although we hoped it wouldn't. But when that day finally did come, I realized in my heart of hearts that I had never seriously thought it would. When people who were a part of your life, as well as of the country, for so many years and in such a profound way, suddenly die, you feel a terrible sense of loss. I can hardly remember what my life was like before Silvio Berlusconi became a leading figure on the public scene. And in recent years, after a series of ups and downs, our relationship had become the one I had always hoped to have with him. We spoke often, he would give me lots of good advice. I always told him what I thought, and I'm sure that he was pleased with the government's and our successes. He considered them to be his own, and they were. I remember the last time I saw him, when I went to see him at the San Raffaele Hospital. When I got there, he was lying in his bed. It looked like he was in pain, but as soon as he saw me, he got up on his feet and started making plans for the next European elections. I realized that what had inspired him all his life was the motivation, the ability to always set himself a new goal, to think big. The last time I heard from him was the first day of a trip to Tunisia, and in that case as well his advice had been very useful. I told him I would visit him again the following week, but I never made it. He was a huge loss for us, but we'll do our best to continue to make him proud of what we've built together.

Do you ever feel lonely?

My relationship with loneliness is perhaps my biggest problem. Because, on the one hand, you can never be alone when you're surrounded by people morning, noon, and night; but on the other, the people who are always around you are mostly there to act as a filter for all the others. And when you worry about being able to answer every single text message, and when you do answer about how those innocent, or hastily written, or friendly, or nervous words can be used against you, you realize that the job is cutting you off from the rest of the world. And even if you are the same person you were before, you realize that others—even those you've known you all your life—look at you differently. A few weeks ago, three of my oldest friends came to see me at Palazzo Chigi. They were excited about surprising me, but when they came into my office, they looked petrified. They were anxious, that was my perception of them there. As if there were suddenly a barrier between us, especially due to the solemnity of the place and the role. To them I was no longer Giorgia; I was the Prime Minister. In other words, a typical situation in which appearance can be deceptive. I was forced to break the ice: "Hey guys, what are you doing just standing there, I'm not going to question you, or anything like that." It made me think, and it also made me feel alone.

A few Sundays ago, I was following you in the news agency reports. At a certain point I thought there was a mistake because one minute you were in Pompeii, and the next you were in Tunisia. How do you keep up?

As long as you keep moving [*laughs*]. But that's the least of it. The Good Lord fortunately gave me a decent amount of physical resistance. The problem is managing to sleep enough, because when you get back at ten o'clock at night—if you're lucky—and have dinner at eleven p.m., you end up going to bed late. But the next morning, the alarm still goes off at dawn, especially when Ginevra goes to school. I try to be the one who always wakes her up in the morning, just as I do my best to tuck her in at night. It's our time together.

That was my next question for you. How do you deal with Ginevra?

That is no doubt the hardest part. At the age of six she needs her mother, and I'm hardly ever there. Ginevra is an intelligent, independent little girl, and she tries not to complain. But the last few months have been a lot for her. Every now and then, with the straightforwardness that is typical of children, she says something that makes your heart shrink to the size of a peanut. A few weeks ago, she saw me packing yet another suitcase, ready to go, and started crying. She kept saying over and over again: "My friends are always with their Mamma, and I never am!" I felt like jumping out the window. Sometimes she'll ask: "Mamma, why did you pick this job?" In other words, it can be really hard. But there are also times when she does things that pay you back for everything. When I traveled to Washington, she was with me. After my meetings with the US Congress and the bilateral meeting at the White House, that evening we went to dinner with the Italian Embassy staff and officers. At a certain point I got up to propose a toast to thank them all for their work. Then the ambassador also got up and proposed a toast. At which point Ginevra said: "Mamma, I want to say something, too, but I'm too shy." So, I said, "I'll stand up with you if you want." She mustered up the courage, took my hand, and stood up on the chair. The room grew quiet waiting to hear what she had to say. "Mamma, I love you," were her words. It was a moment of absolute bliss. Many of the people who love me say that one day she will understand that the time I wasn't with her was also time I dedicated to her. But I'm not sure that's how it will be. I hope so, of course. In any case, Ginevra is the tip of the iceberg of a problem that everyone who loves me has. Even Andrea complains, and rightly so, that we're never alone, we can never do anything together, we can't have a normal life. The other day my sister Arianna told me that she dreamed we were at some event and that she couldn't reach me. You don't need Freud to understand the meaning of that dream. My mother complains that I never call her, my friends never see me anymore. It's the truth, unfortunately, but in the end I'm the one who's paying the highest price of all. When someone says "I miss you," I often reply, "I miss myself, too."

You've been criticized for taking Ginevra with you on international missions.

What else is new? Whatever I do is controversial, but, again, I don't care. Ginevra will always be with me, whenever I can take her; people can say what they want. I don't think that how I decide to raise my daughter is anyone's business, and the fact that I take her with me doesn't mean I'm not doing my job. Any who sticks their nose into my relationship with my daughter is just being mean, and I never give any importance to people who are mean.

How do you spend your free time?

Free time? What's that? Look, the little amount of time I force myself to take off I spend with Ginevra. If she's not around, maybe she's at some birthday party or playing with her friends, then like all the woman of my age these days I play rummy, with my neighbors in particular. My condominium is like a commune where we go from one apartment to another in our pajamas, and the children take turns going from one apartment to another to play. Rummy is easy to learn but hard to play well, especially in its international version, so it's a game that forces you to focus. This means it helps you to forget your worries. This is harder for me to do if I'm watching TV. I've often watched a movie and then realized toward the end that I was hardly watching it because of all the problems I kept thinking about.

Do you sleep well?

Let's say I manage to sleep, even though, as I said, I always sleep very little. Sometimes I wake up in the middle of the night thinking I've found the solution to a problem. I'll get up, jot it down, and then go back to sleep. In the morning, when I read what I wrote, it always seems surreal. But it makes you realize that your brain keeps working even while you're asleep.

What do you think needs to be improved compared to these first few months of government?

I hope to be able to bring more order. The first months were very hectic—we found ourselves in the spin cycle of a washing machine we didn't fully know how to operate. Now things are clearer to me, I can recognize the priorities, and I think I can plan the work better. I want to schedule the government's measures over the five-year term to make sure we fulfill the pledges we made to the Italian people. I hope to be able to recharge my batteries in August, something I desperately need to do.

Where do you see yourself in ten years' time?

I can tell you how I *hope* to see myself in ten years' time: proud of how I did my job, and knowing that it wasn't done in vain.

Epilogue

"Why, to think of it, we're in the same tale still! It's going on. Don't the great tales never end?"
"No, they never end as tales," said Frodo. "But the people in them come, and go when their part's ended. Our part will end later—or sooner."

—J. R. R. Tolkien, *The Two Towers*

"We've reached the end of our adventure," says Giorgia Meloni at our final meeting, closing the ever-present notebook in which she jots down notes and reflections. And yet, "Meloni's workshop," which remained active day and night even during the weeks of our conversations, are like every great tale—it cannot truly come to an end, as Tolkien says in what is widely known as her favorite novel.

"My story is not that of a rabbit pulled out of a hat in this post-ideological era, where politics is sometimes confused with a sideshow. It's the story of a solid, ancient political identity that has passed through generations—and, we hope, will pass through many more. The vision I represent today was not born with me, and it will not end with me. My task is to pave my stretch of the road and then pass the baton to others who will carry on the same task."

That is her main strength: the awareness that she does not represent only herself—that she has been given an opportunity that others have not—but that she can repay the sacrifices of many. She knows the road ahead won't be smooth, that there will be many events and unforeseen challenges that may slow her down, force her to speed up, or even change course. She knows her goal is clear, but that the road cannot always be traveled at the speed or within the time frame she had set herself. Every day brings something new—and sometimes, pain.

What stands out about Giorgia Meloni is her total lack of fear—at least in the sense meant by Giovanni Falcone: "The important thing is not establishing," the judge wrote, "if you are afraid or not, but it's to be able to live with your own fear without being influenced by it. Otherwise it's not courage anymore, but recklessness." The Prime Minister comes across as approachable, polite, and generous with her time. Despite her position, she makes an effort to put everyone at ease—at least, that was my experience—and to make complex things seem simple. But behind that facade is a woman of determination. One who is unflinching when it comes to herself—both in work and in life.

During one of our meetings, she was suffering from a high fever. When I suggested we postpone our interview to when she felt better, she cut me off with a hoarse voice: "When I make a commitment I keep it. Let's continue." It was the last word on the matter.

This long interview was not conceived to oppose Giorgia's ideas—something legitimately done daily by the press and media in general, though not always in a fair or transparent manner—but rather to understand her, to sum up her way of being and put it in some form of order. Giorgia's "vision" of things is neither gospel nor testament, and the word "vision"—which she deliberately chose for this book—is the key here. These pages are not meant to deliver absolute truths that must be shared. They offer her authentic vision of life and the world—unfiltered by external judgments or prejudices—expressed through a political project that she is carrying forward, together with allies old and new. A project she is submitting—so far successfully—for the judgment of the Italian people and the ultimate empirical test, which remains the only truly impartial judge.

During the weeks I conducted these interviews, I witnessed firsthand—and in real time—several events that later made headlines during the early months of Meloni's government. Some of them are not recounted here—not out of discretion, but because they belong to the daily news cycle, not the deeper story we set out to tell. In any case, I never had the sense that, no matter how unpleasant or awkward a situation, Giorgia Meloni was particularly fazed—contrary to what was being written day after day in the press. At most, she was annoyed by the background noise that interfered with the main score of her playbook.

Through this unique opportunity—one I am grateful for, and one I hope I have managed to convey to the reader—I came to know a woman who is both significant and compelling. A woman who understands that if you have an idea and truly believe in it, you won't please everyone. That being misunderstood is part of the cost. That solitude becomes a fact of life. And that, in the words of Margaret Thatcher, "A man may climb Everest for himself, but at the summit he plants his country's flag."

Freedom and Democracy

The first speech given by Prime Minister Giorgia Meloni in the Chamber of Deputies on October 25, 2022.

Mr. President, honorable colleagues,

I have spoken many times in this House, as a Member of Parliament, as Vice-President of the House, as Minister of Youth; yet the solemnity here is so great that I have never been able to speak without a feeling of emotion and deep respect. This is all the more true today that I am addressing you in my capacity as Prime Minister, asking you to express your confidence in a government under my leadership. It is a great responsibility for those who must earn and deserve that trust, and a great responsibility for those who must grant or deny it. These are the fundamental moments of our democracy, to which we must never become accustomed. That is why the first people I want to thank are all those who will speak out in this House according to their own beliefs, whatever decisions they may make.

I wish to express my sincerest gratitude to the President of the Republic, Sergio Mattarella, who, in following up on the choice clearly made by the Italians last September 25, gave me some precious advice. I am also grateful to the parties in the governing coalition, to my Brothers of Italy, to the League, Forza Italia, Noi Moderati, and to their leaders, to the

Center-Right that, after asserting itself at the ballot box, has given birth to this government in one of the shortest periods of time in the history of the Republic. I believe that this is the most tangible sign of a cohesion that, when put to the test, always manages to overcome different sensibilities in the name of a higher interest. The speed of these past days was only natural for us, but it was also our duty, because the very difficult condition in which Italy finds itself does not allow us to hesitate or waste time, and we do not intend to do so. And I also want to thank my predecessor, Prime Minister Mario Draghi, who, both nationally and internationally, in recent weeks, did everything he could to ensure the quick and peaceful transition of power to the new government, of course, even though, ironically, that government was led by the president of the only opposition party to the executive that he chaired. A lot has been said about this, but I wish to emphasize that there is nothing unusual about it. This is how it should always be, this is how it is in great democracies.

And, among the many burdens I feel weighing on my shoulders today, there is that of being the first woman to head the government of this nation. When I reflect on the magnitude of this fact, I inevitably find myself thinking of the responsibility I have to all those women who at this time face great and unfair difficulties in asserting their talents or, more bluntly, their right to see the appreciation of the sacrifices they make each and every day. But I also think, with reverence, to the women who, with their example, have built the ladder that has allowed me to reach and break the heavy crystal ceiling over our heads today. Women like Cristina Trivulzio di Belgioioso, an elegant organizer of both salons and barricades. Or Rosalie Montmasson, who was stubborn enough to leave with Garibaldi's Expedition of the Thousand that made this country. Like Alfonsina Strada, who worked hard to defeat the winds of prejudice. Like Maria Montessori or Grazia Deledda, who by their example opened wide the gates of education to girls all over the country. Not to mention Tina Anselmi, Nilde Jotti, Rita Levi Montalcini, Oriana Fallaci, Ilaria Alpi, Mariagrazia Cutuli, Fabiola Giannotti, Marta Cartabia, Elisabetta Casellati, Samantha Cristoforetti, Chiara Corbella Petrillo. Thank you all! Thank you for demonstrating the value of Italian women, something I hope to be able to do as well.

However, my most heartfelt thanks go to the Italian people, to those who chose not to skip this election so they could cast their vote, thus allowing for the fulfillment of this path to democracy, which sees the people, and only the people, as the holders of sovereignty; with regret, however, for all those who have relinquished the exercise of their civic duty that is enshrined in the Constitution, citizens who increasingly feel their vote is useless, because, they say: "Someone else will decide anyway; everything is always decided in the government buildings, or in exclusive circles." Unfortunately, this has often been the case over the past eleven years, with a series of government majorities that are fully and constitutionally legitimate, yet dramatically distant from the voters' wishes.

Today, our intention is to disrupt this Italian anomaly, by giving birth to a political government that is fully representative of the will of the people. And we intend to do so by fully assuming the rights and duties incumbent upon those who win elections: i.e., to be a parliamentary majority and government team for five years, doing so to the best of our ability, always putting the nation's interest before partisan and party interests. We will not use the vote of millions of Italians to replace one system of power with another different and opposing one.

What we want to do is to unleash this nation's finest energy, and guarantee Italians, all Italians, a future of greater freedom, justice, well-being, and security. And if in order to do that we have to displease some of the powers that be or make choices that may not be immediately understood by some of the citizens, we will not back down, because courage does not fail us.

We went into the election campaign with a coalition government framework program and with more articulated programs from the individual parties. The voters chose the Center-Right and, within the coalition, they rewarded certain proposals more than others. We will uphold those commitments, because the bond between the representative and the represented lies at the very heart of democracy. I am well aware that some observers and opposition political forces will not like many of our proposals, but I do not intend to go along with the tendency according to which democracy belongs to some more than to others, and that an undesirable election outcome should not be accepted and should, indeed, be prevented from being realized, by whatever means. In recent days there have been several people, even outside our national borders, who have said that they want to keep an eye on the new government. I would suggest that they find a better way to spend their time. There are good and embattled opposition forces in this House and in our Parliament, which are more than capable of making their voices heard, without—I hope—any outside help.

I would hope that those forces agree with me that those from abroad who also say they want to keep an eye Italy are not disrespecting me or this government: they are disrespecting the Italian people, who do not need to be taught anything.

Italy is rightfully part of the West and its alliance system, a founding state of the European Union, the eurozone, and the Atlantic Alliance, a member of the G7, and, even before all this, the cradle, together with Greece, of Western civilization and its value system, founded on freedom, equality, and democracy, precious fruits born of Europe's Classical and Judeo-Christian roots. We are the heirs of Saint Benedict, an Italian, and the patron saint of all of Europe.

Europe. Allow me, on the topic of Europe, to first of all thank the leaders of the EU institutions, the President of the European Council, Charles Michel, the President of the Commission, Ursula von der Leyen, the President of the European Parliament, Roberta Metsola, the Acting President of the Council of the European Union, my friend Petr Fiala, as well as the many heads of state and government who, in these hours, have wished me well in my work. Of course, I am not unaware of the curiosity and interest in the stance that the government will adopt toward the European institutions or, even better, I would like to say within the European institutions, because that is where Italy will make its voice heard, as befits a great founding member state of the European Community. Not to hold back or sabotage European integration, as I have sometimes heard, even in recent weeks, but to help steer it toward greater effectiveness in responding to crises and outside threats, and toward an approach closer to the citizens and businesses.

To put it bluntly, we do not conceive of the European Union as an exclusive club, with first-class and second-class members or, worse still, as a corporation limited by shares and run by a board of directors, whose sole task is to keep the books in order. For us, the European Union is the common home of the European peoples and, as such, it must be able to meet the greatest challenges of our time, starting with those that the member states can hardly face alone. I am thinking of trade agreements of course, but also of the supply of raw materials and energy, of migration policies, of geopolitical choices, of the fight against terrorism, major challenges for which the European Union has not always been ready.

Because, my fellow members of Parliament, how can it be that an organization that was born in 1950, seventy years ago, to integrate Europe's coal and steel industries into a single market known as the Coal and Steel Economic Community, now finds itself, after having expanded its spheres of competence by leaps and bounds, to be more vulnerable precisely in the area of energy supply and raw materials?

Those who ask these questions are neither enemies nor heretics; rather, they are pragmatists who are not afraid to say when something is not working as well as it could. What is needed is a more effective integration that can face up to the great challenges, in keeping with the founding motto that reads, "United in diversity"; for that is what distinguishes Europe, a group of nations each with thousands of years of history, capable of coming together while bringing their own identity as an added value. A European home in common no doubt means shared rules in the economic-financial sphere as well. This government will respect the rules that are currently in force and, at the same time, offer its contribution to change the ones that have not worked, starting with the ongoing debate on the reform of the Stability and Growth Pact.

Because of its strength and its history, Italy has the duty, even before the right, to stand tall in these international forums, with a constructive spirit, but without subordination, without inferiority complexes, as has too often seemed to occur in the past, combining the assertion of its national interest with an awareness of a common European and Western destiny.

The Atlantic Alliance guarantees our democracies a framework of peace and security that we all too often take for granted. It is Italy's duty to contribute to it fully, because, whether we like it or not, freedom has a cost, and that cost, for a country, is the ability to defend itself and the reliability it demonstrates within the framework of the alliances that it is a part of. Over the years, Italy has been able to demonstrate this, starting with the many international missions in which we have played a major role; for this I wish to thank the women and men of our Armed Forces for holding up high Italy's prestige in the most difficult situations, even if it means sacrificing their lives to do so: your country will always be grateful to you!

Italy will continue to be a reliable partner in the Atlantic Alliance, starting with our support of the valiant Ukrainian people who oppose the invasion by the Russian Federation, not only because we cannot accept a war of aggression and the violation of the territorial integrity of a sovereign nation, but also because it is the best way to defend our own national interest. Only an Italy that honors its commitments can have the authority to ask, in Europe and in the West in general, that the burdens of this international crisis be shared in a more balanced way. That is, in fact, what we intend to do, starting with the issue of energy.

The war has exacerbated the already very difficult situation caused by increases in energy and fuel costs, costs that are unsustainable for many businesses that may be forced to close and lay off their workers, and for millions of families who are already unable to cope with rising energy bills. But anyone who believes that it is possible to trade Ukraine's freedom for our own peace of mind is wrong. Giving in to Putin's blackmail on energy would not solve the problem, it would exacerbate it, paving the way for further demands and more blackmail, with future energy increases even greater than those we have experienced in recent months.

The signals that came from the last European Council represent a step forward achieved, also thanks to the efforts of my predecessor and Energy Minister Cingolani. But they are still not enough. The absence still today of a common response leaves—as the only outlet—measures by individual national governments that risk undermining the domestic market and the competitiveness of our companies.

As concerns prices, while it is true that the mere discussion of containment measures has momentarily curbed speculation, it is clear that if announcements are not quickly followed up with concrete mechanisms, then speculation will resume. This is also why it will be necessary to maintain and strengthen national measures to support families and businesses, as concerns both bills and fuel, a massive financial commitment that will drain a large part of the resources available and force us to postpone other measures that we would have liked to initiate as early as the next budget law. But our priority today must be to curb the high cost of energy, and accelerate, using every means possible, the diversification of sources of supply and domestic production. Because I would like to believe that the tragedy of the energy crisis can also, paradoxically, become an opportunity for Italy. Our seas possess natural gas fields that we have a duty to fully exploit, and our country, particularly the South, is a paradise for renewables, with its sun, wind, the heat of the earth, tides, rivers, a wealth of green energy too often hindered by bureaucracy and vetoes that are hard to understand. In short, I am convinced that Italy, with a little courage and practical spirit, could emerge from this crisis stronger and more independent than before.

In addition to high energy prices, Italian households are facing a level of inflation that has reached 11.1 percent annually, and is inexorably eroding their purchasing power, despite the fact that some of these increases have been absorbed by companies. It is essential to intervene with measures aimed at increasing families' disposable income, starting by reducing taxes on productivity bonuses, further raising the exemption threshold for so-called fringe benefits, enhancing corporate welfare, succeeding in broadening the range of primary goods that enjoy reduced VAT at 5 percent. Concrete measures that we will also address with the next budget law, on which we are already hard at work.

The context in which the government will find itself operating is a very complex one, perhaps the most difficult one since World War II. Geopolitical tensions and the energy crisis are holding back hopes for a post-pandemic economic recovery. Macroeconomic forecasts for 2023 indicate a marked slowdown in the Italian, European, and world economies, moreover, in a climate of absolute uncertainty. In September, the European Central Bank revised its 2023 growth forecast for the eurozone, cutting its June forecast by as much as 1.2 percentage points, predicting growth equal to just 0.9 percent. A slowdown and downward revisions that also obviously affect the performance of the Italian economy for next year. In the latest update note to the Economic and Financial Document (DEF), the GDP growth forecast for 2023 stalls at 0.6 percent, exactly a quarter of the 2.4 percent forecast in the April EDEF, and the Ministry of Finance's forecasts are actually optimistic as compared with the International Monetary Fund's most recent ones, according to which 2023 will be a year of recession for the Italian economy: minus 0.2 percent, the worst result among the world's major economies after Germany's. And this is not, unfortunately, an isolated economic situation—the data speaks volumes. Over the past two decades, Italy has grown by a total of 4 percent, France and Germany by more than 20 percent; in the past ten years, our nation has ranked in the last places in Europe for economic and employment growth, with the sole exception of the rebound recorded after the GDP collapse in 2020. It is no accident that those were ten years during which the country had a series of weak, heterogeneous governments without a clear popular mandate, incapable of resolving the structural deficiencies that this country and its economy suffer from, nor of laying the foundations for sustained and lasting growth.

Low or zero growth, therefore, accompanied by a surge in inflation that has exceeded 9 percent in the eurozone and prompted the European Central Bank, like other central banks, to raise interest rates for the first time in eleven years. A decision considered by many to be risky and likely to affect bank lending to households and businesses, and which comes on top of the one already made by the same central bank to end as of July 1, 2022, the program to purchase fixed-income securities on the open market, creating additional difficulty for those member states that, like ours, have a high public debt. We are therefore in the midst of a storm. Our boat has suffered some severe damage, and the Italians have entrusted us with the task of steering the ship into port on this very difficult crossing. We were aware of what was ahead of us, as are all the other political forces, even those who, governing in the last ten years, have brought—because this is what the numbers say—a worsening of the main macroeconomic fundamentals. Today they will without a doubt say that they have the solution and are ready to blame the new government for the difficulties Italy is facing. We were well aware of the burden we would be carrying on our shoulders. But we still fought to assume this responsibility because, first, we are not people accustomed to running away, and, second, because our ship, Italy, with all its imperfections, remains "the most beautiful ship in the world," to quote the words famously used by the American aircraft carrier *Independence* when it first came upon the *Amerigo Vespucci* training ship. A solid vessel to which no destination is precluded if it decides to resume its voyage. So we are here to try to mend the sails that have been torn, repair the wood of the hull, and overcome the waves that break over us, with the compass of our beliefs to show us the route to our chosen destination and with a crew that is capable of performing its duties to the best of its ability.

We have been asked how we intend to appease investors when faced with a debt at 145 percent of GDP, second in Europe only to that of Greece. We could answer by citing some of our economy's fundaments that remain solid in spite of everything: we are among the few European nations in constant primary surplus, that is, the state spends less than it collects, net of interest on debt. The private savings of Italian households have passed the 5 trillion euro threshold and in a climate of confidence could support investment in the real economy. But even more important than these figures, which are already significant, is Italy's still untapped potential. I am tempted to say that, if this government succeeds in doing what it intends to do, then taking a chance on Italy might not just be a safe investment, but maybe even a good deal, because the horizon we want to look toward is not next year or the next election deadline. What we are interested in is what Italy will look like ten years from now, and I am prepared to do what needs to be done, at the cost of not being understood, even at the cost of not being reelected, to make sure that I, through my work and our work, have made the future of this nation a better one.

The way to reduce debt is not through the blind austerity that was imposed in the past, nor is it through more or less creative financial speculation. The high road, the only one possible, is economic growth that is both lasting and structural.

And to achieve it, we are, of course, open to encouraging foreign investments: if, on the one hand, we will come across predatory attitudes that jeopardize strategic national production, on the other hand, we will be open to welcoming and stimulating those foreign companies that choose to invest in Italy, bringing development, employment and know-how, according to a logic of mutual benefits.

This is the context for the National Recovery and Resilience Plan (NRRP). Funds raised through the issuance of common European bonds to cope with global crises. A proposal that was made in the past by the Center-Right government, with the then-Minister Giulio Tremonti, for years opposed, sometimes mocked, then implemented. The NRRP is an extraordinary opportunity to modernize Italy: we all have a duty to make the most of it. The challenge is tricky because of the structural and bureaucratic constraints that have always made it hard for Italy to be able to fully use even European funds from ordinary programming. Suffice to consider that the supplement for the 2022 DEF reduced public spending triggered by the NRRP to 15 billion as compared with the 29.4 projected in last April's DEF. Meeting future deadlines will require even more attention, considering that, so far, we have mostly accounted for works that have already been started in the past, something that cannot continue to be done in the coming years. We will spend the 68.9 billion in grants and the 122.6 billion loaned to Italy by the Next Generation EU as best as we can, without delay and without waste, agreeing with the European Commission on the necessary adjustments to optimize spending, especially against the background of rising commodity prices and the energy crisis. For these matters are addressed with a pragmatic approach and not an ideological one.

The NRRP should be viewed not only as a major public spending plan, but as an opportunity to make a real cultural shift. To finally shelve the logic of bonuses, for some, often mainly of use for electoral campaigns, in favor of medium-term investments aimed at the welfare of the entire national community. Remove all obstacles that hold back economic growth and that we have too long resigned ourselves to considering endemic ills of Italy, but are not.

One of these is undoubtedly political instability. For the past twenty years, Italy has had, on average, a government every two years, often changing the governing majority as well. This is the reason why measures that guaranteed definite and immediate approval have always prevailed over strategic choices. It is the reason why bureaucracies have often become untouchable and immune to merit. It is the reason why Italy's ability to negotiate in international bodies has been weak. And it is the reason why foreign investments, which resent the volatility of governments, has been discouraged. It is the reason why we firmly believe that Italy needs a constitutional reform in a presidential direction, one that guarantees stability and restores centrality to popular sovereignty. A reform that enables Italy to move from being an "interlocutory democracy" to a "deciding democracy."

We want to start with the hypothesis of semi-presidentialism based on the French model, which in the past had also won wide approval from the Center-Left. However, we remain open to other solutions as well.

We wish to discuss this with all the political forces in Parliament, to arrive at the best and most shared reform possible. But let it be clear that we will not give up reforming Italy if we are faced with prejudicial opposition. If that is the case, we will move according to the mandate given to us on this issue by the Italians: to give Italy an institutional system in which whoever wins will govern for five years and at the end will be judged by the voters for what he or she has managed to do.

Alongside presidential reform, we will follow up on the positive process of differentiated autonomy that has already been initiated by several Italian regions according to constitutional provisions and in the application of the principles of subsidiarity and solidarity, within a framework of national cohesion. For the province of Bolzano, we will deal with the restoration of the standards of autonomy that led to the release of the UN discharge in 1992. It is our intention to complete the process in order to give the City of Rome Capital the powers and resources that befit a great European capital, and to bestow a new centrality on our municipalities. Because every *campanile*, or bell tower, every *borgo*, or village, is a piece of our identity to be defended. I am thinking in particular of those in inland areas, mountainous areas, and highlands, which need a state that is an ally and will help in fostering residency and fighting depopulation.

I am convinced that the turning point we have in mind is also the best opportunity to return to putting the Southern Question at the center of the Italian agenda. The South is no longer seen as a problem, but, rather, as an opportunity for development for the entire nation.

We will work hard to close an unacceptable infrastructure gap, eliminate disparities, create jobs, ensure social security, and improve the quality of life. We must succeed in ending the paradox whereby the South exports labor, intelligence, and capital, all of which are crucial to the very regions that provide them. It will not be an easy task, of course, but our commitment will be total.

And if infrastructure in the South can no longer be postponed, new infrastructure needs to be built in the rest of Italy as well, to enhance connections for people and goods, but also for data and communications. With the goal of connecting not just the North to the South, but the Tyrrhenian coast to the Adriatic coast, and the islands to the rest of the peninsula as well.

Structural investments are needed to deal with the climate crisis, environmental challenges, hydrogeological risk, and shoreline retreat, and to accelerate the reconstruction processes of the territories affected in recent years by earthquakes and natural disasters, such as the dramatic flooding that devastated the Marche region on the night of September 15–16. Please allow me, together with all of you, to once again offer our condolences for the victims and our sympathy for the entire community: we are with you, we will not abandon you, you can count on us.

We intend to protect national strategic infrastructure by ensuring the public ownership of networks, on which companies will be able to offer services under free competition, starting with communications. Digital transition, strongly supported by the NRRP, must go hand in hand with technological sovereignty, national cloud, and cybersecurity.

And we finally want to introduce a national interest safeguard clause, in economic terms as well, for public infrastructure concessions, such as highways and airports. Because the model featuring oligarchs sitting on oil wells accumulating billions without even making investments is not a free-market model worthy of a Western democracy.

Italy must return to having an industrial policy, focusing on those sectors in which it can count on a competitive advantage. I am thinking of the brand, which is made up of fashion, luxury, design, all the way to high technology. It is made up of products of absolute excellence in agribusiness, which must be defended in Europe and with greater integration of the supply chain at the national level, also to aspire to a full food sovereignty that can no longer be postponed. Which does not mean, of course, putting pineapples out of business, as some have said, but more trivially ensuring that we will not depend on faraway nations to feed our children. I think of Italy's favorable position in the Mediterranean and the opportunities related to the maritime economy, which can and must become a strategic asset for the whole of Italy and in particular for the development of the South. And I think of beauty.

Yes, because Italy is the nation that more than any other in the world encapsulates the idea of landscape, artistic, narrative, expressive beauty.

The whole world knows it, loves us for it, and that is why they want to buy Italian, learn about our history, and vacation here. It is a source of pride, but more importantly it is an invaluable economic resource that fuels our tourist and cultural industry. And I would add that going back to focus on the strategic value of being Italian also means promoting the Italian language abroad and enhancing the link with the Italian communities in every part of the world that are an integral part of ours.

For all the growth objectives to be achieved, a cultural revolution is needed in the relationship between the state and the production system, which must be equal and based on mutual trust. Those who have the strength and will to do business in Italy today should be supported and facilitated, not harassed and looked upon with suspicion, because wealth is created by companies with their workers, not by the state with decrees or edicts. The motto of this government will be "Do not disturb those who want to get things done."

Businesses are above all asking for less bureaucracy, clear and certain rules, and quick and transparent responses. We will tackle the problem starting with a structural simplification and deregulation of administrative procedures in order to give a boost to the economy, growth, and investment, not least because we all know how excessive legislation, red tape, and regulation exponentially increase the risk of irregularities, litigation, and corruption. An evil that we have a duty to eradicate.

We need fewer, clearer rules for everyone and a new relationship between the citizens and the public administration; so that citizens won't feel like the weaker party that is forced to face a tyrannical state that doesn't listen to their needs and frustrates their expectations.

From this Copernican revolution, a new fiscal pact must emerge, based on three pillars. The first one involves reducing the tax burden on businesses and families through a reform guided by fairness. I am thinking, for example, of the gradual introduction of the so-called "quoziente familiare" [*"family quotient," i.e. the calculation of the taxes to be paid based on the number of family members—Translator's Note*], but also of extending the flat rate taxation for the self-employed from the current

65,000 euros to 100,000 euros in revenue. Alongside this, I propose the introduction of a flat tax on income increases compared to the highest income achieved in the previous three years—a virtuous measure, with a limited impact on the State's finances, that could serve as a strong growth incentive.

The second pillar involved a tax truce to allow citizens and businesses, particularly small- and medium-sized enterprises, that are struggling to settle their accounts with the tax authorities.

And, finally, a hard battle against tax evasion, which must begin with total evaders, large companies, and large-scale VAT fraud. Most importantly, it must be a real fight against evasion, not just a hunt for revenue. That is why we will start with an adjustment of the evaluation criteria for the Internal Revenue Agency's results, anchoring them to the actual amounts collected, not merely to the number of unpaid tax reports, as has been the case until now.

Businesses and workers have long been calling for the reduction of the tax and contribution wedge as an undeferrable priority. The excessive tax burden on labor is one of the main obstacles to the creation of new jobs and the competitiveness of our companies in international markets. Our goal is to intervene gradually to arrive at a cut of at least five points in the wedge in favor of businesses and workers, in order to lighten the tax burden of the former and increase the paychecks of the latter. To incentivize companies to hire, we have in mind a tax mechanism that rewards labor-intensive activities—"the more you hire the less you pay," is how we summarized it —but of course this must not diminish the necessary support for technological innovation.

Speaking of business and labor, our thoughts turn to the dozens of crisis units still open, to which we will devote our utmost efforts, and to those thousands of self-employed workers who have not been able to get back on their feet since the pandemic. For those who have often been unjustly treated like the children of a lesser God, we wish to recognize suitable protections, in line with the ones that are rightly guaranteed to employees. Because we have always stood by those nearly five million self-employed workers, including artisans, store owners, and freelancers, who are one of the backbones of the Italian economy, and we will not stop now. For us, a worker is a worker.

Adequate safeguards must also be recognized for those who retire, or would like to retire, after a lifetime of work. We intend to ease exit flexibility with mechanisms that are compatible with the viability of the pension system, starting, with the limited time available for the next budget law, with the renewal of the measures set to expire at the end of the year. However, the priority for the future must be a pension system that also ensures security for younger generations and for those who will receive their pension solely based on their actual national insurance contributions. This is a social time bomb that we continue to ignore, but in the future, it will affect millions of workers who will find themselves with pensions that are even lower than the ones—already too low—being paid out today.

There is an issue of rampant poverty that we cannot ignore. His Holiness Pope Francis, to whom I extend my fondest greetings, recently underscored an important concept: "Poverty," he said, "is not fought with welfarism; what gives dignity is work." This is a profound truth that only those who have experienced poverty from up close can truly appreciate. This is the road we intend to take: we want to maintain and, where possible, improve economic support for those who are truly weak and cannot work. Struggling retirees, the disabled, whose protection must be increased in every way possible, those who don't have an income but who have young children to take care of—all these categories come to mind. None of them will be denied the help from the state that they are due. But for the others, for those who are able to work, the solution cannot be citizens' income. That solution can only be work, training, and accompanying them to work, also taking full advantage of the resources and possibilities made available by the European Social Fund. Citizens' income, because of the way it was conceived and implemented, has proven to be a defeat for those who would have been able to do their part for Italy, as well as for themselves and their families.

And while there are different positions on citizens' income in this House, I am sure we all agree on the importance of ending the tragedy of work-related accidents and occupational fatalities. It is not a question of introducing new regulations, but, rather, of guaranteeing the full application of those that already exist. The labor union has reminded us over and over again, and most recently with the demonstration that was held this past Saturday, we cannot accept the idea that an eighteen-year-old like Giuliano De Seta—who represents every victim of work-related deaths—can leave home for work never to return.

We need to bridge the large gap between education and the skills required by the labor market with specific training paths, certainly, but even before that via school and university training that is more focused on the dynamics of the labor market. Education is the most formidable tool for increasing a nation's wealth, in all respects, because material capital is nothing if there is no human capital as well.

This is why schools and universities will once again be crucial to any action taken by the government; they represent a fundamental strategic resource for Italy, its future, and its young people. Our intention to restore the correlation between education and merit has led to a great deal of debate. Frankly, I am impressed. Studies show how, today, those who come from an affluent family have the opportunity to make up for the shortcomings of a school system that has been going downhill, while students with fewer resources are harmed by education that does not reward merit, because no one else will fill those gaps.

Italy is not a country for young people. Over time, our society has become increasingly disinterested in their future, in the widespread phenomenon of young people excluding themselves from the educational and work cycle, as well as in the deviant behavior that has increasingly become an emergency, behavior that involves drug use, alcoholism, and crime. The pandemic only made things worse, and faced with this scenario, in recent months, some politicians have found the only solution to be free cannabis for everyone, because for them it was the easiest answer. Our plan is to work on helping young people to grow all around; to promote artistic and cultural activities, as well as sports, an extraordinary tool that promotes sociality, development, and well-being; to work on schooling, mostly entrusted to the self-sacrifice and talent of our teachers, who are often left alone to navigate in a sea of structural, technological, and motivational deficiencies; to guarantee decent salaries and protections, scholarships for those who deserve them, to encourage business culture and honor loans. We owe it to these young people, from whom we have taken away everything, leaving them only with debts to pay back! And we owe it to Italy, which 161 years ago was unified by the young heroes of the Risorgimento and which today, thanks to the enthusiasm and courage of its young people, can and must be rebuilt!

We know that young people especially care about protecting the natural environment. That will be one of our priorities because, as Roger Scruton, one of the greatest masters of European conservative thought, wrote, "ecology is the most vivid example of the alliance between those who are there, those who have been there, and those who will come after us." Protecting our natural heritage engages us exactly the same way as protecting the heritage of culture, traditions, and spirituality that we inherited from our fathers so that we could pass it on to our children. There is no ecologist more convinced than a conservative; but what distinguishes us from certain ideological environmentalism is that we want to defend nature with humans in it, combining environmental, economic, and social sustainability. Accompanying businesses and citizens toward a green transition, without consigning ourselves to new strategic dependencies and respecting the principle of technological neutrality: this will be our approach.

I think I am rather familiar with the universe of youth engagement, a wonderful training ground for life, regardless of the political ideas one chooses to defend and promote. I confess that it will be difficult for me not to feel a surge of sympathy even for those who take to the streets to challenge the policies of our government, because my own experience will inevitably come to mind. I have participated in and organized countless demonstrations in my life, and I believe that that activity has probably taught me more than any other. So, I wish to address the kids who will inevitably take to the streets against us as well. Steve Jobs famously said, "Stay hungry, stay foolish." I would like to add, "Stay free," because in free will lies the greatness of human beings.

There is another important educational institution, besides school and university, that is perhaps the most important of them all. Obviously, it is the family, the primary core of our societies, the cradle of affection and the place where the identity of each of us is formed; we intend to support and protect it and, with it, support the birth rate, which in 2021 was at its lowest since the Unification of Italy; to get out of demographic stagnation and return to producing those years of the future, that demographic GDP we need, we require a massive plan, an economic but also cultural one, in order to rediscover the beauty of parenthood and put the family back at the heart of society. As we said during our campaign, we are committed to increasing the amounts of the universal family allowance and help young couples obtain a mortgage for their first home, while also working progressively for the introduction of the family quotient. And since family projects go hand in hand with work, we want to incentivize women's employment in every way possible, rewarding those companies that adopt policies offering effective solutions that reconcile home-work time, and supporting municipalities that offer free daycare centers that are open until stores and offices close. Italy needs a new intergenerational alliance with the family as its backbone. This alliance must aim to strengthen the bond that unites the generations, children with grandparents, young people with the elderly, who must, in turn, be protected, valorized, and supported, because they represent our roots and our history.

Montesquieu said that "freedom is that good that makes one enjoy the other things." Freedom is the foundation of a true society of opportunity; it is freedom that must guide our actions, the freedom to be, to do, to produce. A Center-Right government will never restrict the existing freedoms of citizens and businesses. We will see, when all is said and done, when it comes to civil rights and abortion as well, who was lying and who was telling the truth in the election campaign about what our real intentions were.

Freedom. Freedom and democracy are the distinctive elements of contemporary European civilization, in which I have always recognized myself and, therefore, even here, in spite of what has been claimed, I have never felt sympathy for or closeness to antidemocratic regimes; for any regime, including fascism, just as I have always considered the racial laws of 1938 the lowest point in Italian history, a stain that will remain on our people forever.

The totalitarianisms of the twentieth century tore apart all of Europe, not just Italy, for more than half a century, in a succession of horrors that affected most European countries. And horror and crimes, whoever it is that commits them, do not deserve any justification whatsoever and are not compensated for by other horrors and other crimes. In the abyss one never gets even: they simply plummet.

At a very young age I experienced the scent of freedom, the anxiety for historical truth and the rejection of any form of abuse of power or discrimination precisely by campaigning in the Italian Democratic Right. A community of men and women that has always acted in the light of day and in full force in our Republican institutions, even in the darkest years of criminalization and political violence, when, in the name of militant anti-fascism, wrenches were used to murder young men. That long phase of human loss perpetuated the hatred of civil war and pushed away a national reconciliation that the Italian democratic right, more than anyone else, had always hoped for.

Since then, the political community I come from has been steadily moving forward, toward a full and conscious historicization of the twentieth century. It has assumed important governmental responsibilities, swearing an oath to the Republican Constitution, as we had the honor of doing again a few hours ago. It has affirmed and embodied, without any ambiguity, the values of liberal democracy, which are the basis of the common identity of the Italian Center-Right and from which we will not deflect an inch. We will fight all forms of racism, anti-Semitism, political violence, and discrimination.

The topic of freedom was also very much discussed during the pandemic. When COVID entered our lives, it led to the deaths of more than 177,000 people in Italy. We mainly have the health personnel, their professionalism and the self-sacrifice with which they saved thousands of lives to thank for being able to emerge from the crisis. Once again, we are grateful to them. I also with to thank the critical services workers, who never stopped, as well as our extraordinary voluntary workers, virtuous representatives of those intermediate entities that we consider vital to society.

While we cannot rule out a new wave of COVID or a new pandemic in the future, we can learn from the past so that we are prepared. Italy adopted the most restrictive measures in all of the West, going so far as to severely restrict the basic freedoms of people and economic activities; in spite of this, it was one of the countries that performed the worst in terms of mortality and contagions. Something didn't work, and I am going to say, as of now, that we will never, under any circumstances, replicate that model.

Accurate information, prevention, and accountability are more effective than coercion, and listening to doctors in the field is more valuable when dealing with real patients than guidelines written by some bureaucrat. Above all, if the citizens are expected to be responsible, then the first to demonstrate their own responsibility are those who require it. There will need to be clarity about what happened during the management of the pandemic crisis: we owe it to those who lost their lives and to those who did not spare themselves in hospital wards, while others made millions with masks and respirators.

Legality will be the guiding star of government action. I got into politics when I was fifteen years old, as many people know by now, in the aftermath of the Via D'Amelio massacre, in which the Mafia killed Judge Paolo Borsellino. I started doing politics driven by the idea that one could not just stand by and watch, that the anger and indignation that followed such an event had to somehow be translated into civic engagement. The path that has led me today to be Prime Minister of Italy stems from the example of that hero. When, after reading the list of ministers, I went to see the President of the Chamber of Deputies Fontana a couple of days ago, I walked into Montecitorio, where I found both at the beginning and at the end of the grand staircase a picture of Paolo Borsellino. Seeing that image of him gave me a feeling of closure.

We will face the cancer that is the Mafia head-on, as we were taught by the many heroes whose courage set an example for every Italian; heroes who refused to avert their gaze or flee even when they knew that their stubbornness would probably lead to their death. Judges, politicians, special security agents, military personnel, ordinary citizens, priests; giants like Giovanni Falcone, Francesca Morvillo, Rosario Livatino, Rocco Chinnici, Pio La Torre, Carlo Alberto Dalla Chiesa, Piersanti Mattarella, Emanuela Loi, Libero Grassi, Don Pino Puglisi, and with them a very long list of men and women we will never forget. The fight against the Mafia will see us at the forefront; this government will always view criminals and mafiosi with contempt and obstinacy!

And legality also means a justice system that works, with effective equality between prosecution and defense, and trials lasting a reasonable length of time, which is not just a question of legal civilization and respect for the citizens' fundamental rights, but of economic growth as well. A slow justice system costs us at least one percentage point of GDP per year, according to the estimates put forward by Bankitalia.

We will make every effort to restore safety for Italian citizens, bringing back the fundamental principle of the certainty of punishment, thanks also to a new prison plan. Since the beginning of this year, there have been seventy-one prison suicides. This is unworthy of a civilized country, and the working conditions of our prison officers are often equally unworthy.

With the same determination, we will also review the reform of the judiciary, to put an end to the politically biased sentencing that undermines the credibility of the Italian judiciary.

And let me say one more thing: we have made a commitment to limit the excess of discretion in juvenile justice, with guaranteed and objective foster care and adoption procedures, so that there will never be another Bibbiano. We intend to fulfill this commitment.

Italians feel the unbearable burden of cities that are not safe, where there is no immediate protection, where the absence of the state is clearly felt. We want to make a commitment to bring citizens closer to the institutions, but also to bring back the physical presence of the state in every city. We want to make safety a hallmark of this government, alongside our law enforcement, whom I wish to thank today for their self-sacrifice, in many cases working in impossible conditions and for a state that has often given the impression of being more sympathetic to those who threaten our safety than to those who risk their lives to guarantee that safety!

Security and legality, of course, are also about the proper management of migration flows. According to a simple principle: in Italy, as in any other serious country, one does not enter illegally; one enters legally, through "flow decrees" [*the number of visas for non-EU citizens who can enter Italy for employment, self-employment, or seasonal work—Translator's Note*].

In these years of grave inability to find the right solutions for the various migration crises, too many men, women and children have died at sea while attempting to reach Italy. Too many times we have said "Never again," only to end up repeating it over and over again. This government wants to pursue a path that has hardly been taken over the years: the arrest of illegal departures, finally interrupting human trafficking in the Mediterranean.

Our intention is still the same, but, if you don't want us to talk about a naval blockade, I'll put it this way: it is our intention to recover the original proposal of the European Union's Sophia naval mission, whose third phase, which was planned and never implemented, involved blocking the departure of boats from North Africa. We intend to propose it at a European level, apply it in agreement with the North African authorities. This will be accompanied by the creation on African soil of hotspots run by international organizations, where we can screen asylum claims and distinguish those who have the right to be received in Europe from those who do not have that right. However, we do not in any way intend to question the right to asylum for those fleeing war and persecution!

All we want to do in relation to the issue of immigration is to make sure that smugglers aren't the ones deciding who enters Italy and who doesn't.

And then there will be one last thing to do, perhaps the most important of them all: to remove the causes that lead migrants, especially the youngest, to leave their land, their cultural roots, and their families to seek a better life in Europe. Next October 27 will mark the sixtieth anniversary of the death of Enrico Mattei, a great Italian who was among the architects of postwar reconstruction, capable of making agreements of mutual convenience with nations all over the world. I believe that Italy should become the promoter of a "Mattei plan" for Africa, a virtuous model of collaboration and growth between the European Union and African nations. This will also counter the danger of the spread of Islamist extremism, especially in the sub-Saharan area. And so we would like to finally gain back Italy's strategic role in the Mediterranean, after years during which the opposite seemed to occur.

My speech is almost finished, dear colleagues, and I thank you for your patience. The government asking the Parliament for its confidence will not be an easy task, due to the seriousness of the choices that we will be asked to make, but also because of the, shall we say, political bias that I often glimpse in the analyses that concern us. I do believe it is in part justified. After all, I am the first woman to become President of the Council of Ministers. I come from a political history that has often been relegated to the margins of republican history, and I did not get there in the arms of a favorable family background or thanks to important friendships. I am the underdog, the outsider, the one who, in order to succeed, must upset all the odds. And that is exactly what I intend to do again, overturn the predictions, with the help of a good team of ministers and undersecretaries, with the trust and support of those who will choose to vote for us, with the criticism that will come from those who will vote against this government, because, at the end of this adventure, I will be interested in only one thing: to know that we have done all we can to give the Italian people a better nation. Sometimes we will succeed, sometimes we will fail, but rest assured that we will not back down, we will not throw in the towel, we will never betray you.

The day our government was sworn into the hands of the head of state marked the liturgical memory of John Paul II, a Pope, a statesman, a saint whom I had the honor of knowing personally. He taught me something fundamental that I have always treasured. "Freedom," he said, "does not consist in doing what we like, but in having the right to do what we should." I have always been a free person, I will always be a free person and, because of that, I intend to do exactly what I have to.

Thank you.

Also Available from Skyhorse Publishing

I Am Giorgia: My Roots, My Principles

Print ISBN: 978-1-5107-8356-0 | Ebook ISBN: 978-1-5107-8357-7

Excerpt from

I AM GIORGIA

My Roots, My Principles

GIORGIA MELONI

Translated by Sylvia Adrian Notini

Introduction

October 19, 2019. Assembled before me in Piazza San Giovanni were thousands of Italians who had traveled to Rome to join our Center-Right protest. They had come to express their "Italian pride" against the formation of the second Conte administration—yet another government that had come to power without heeding the will of the people. The square was a sea of flags waved by the Brothers of Italy, the Lega Nord, and Forza Italia, all blending together in a spirited dance. The crowd was united by its shared purpose: the fight for the right to be heard and to achieve self-determination against those who sought to exploit institutions for their personal gain.

On the massive stage that had been set up for the occasion, I faced 200,000 people, flanked by my allies Silvio Berlusconi and Matteo Salvini. When it was my turn to speak, I addressed the crowd for twenty minutes, speaking from the heart. I had no script, relying instead on my instinct and passion. My tone was that of a political rally, but—as always— I also tried to convey my vision. On that day, I reiterated a theme I had often emphasized at other events: the value of identity. I spoke of the ongoing clash between those who defend identity—like us—and those who seek to wipe it out—our adversaries. I pointed out how all the key pillars of our identity—family, nation, faith, and even gender—were viewed as the enemy. Our identity is under attack, not by coincidence but by deliberate design.

I concluded my speech with these words: "I am Giorgia. I am a woman, a mother, an Italian, a Christian. You will *never* take that away from me." There was a roar of applause from the people in the square, and the event was a resounding success. But I could never have anticipated the lasting impact those words would have in the months to come.

In the days that followed, my phone was flooded with a curious remix of my speech from different sources. The broadcaster and writer Tommaso Zorzi (who would later win Italy's version of the reality show *Big Brother*) had posted a critical commentary on Instagram. Meanwhile, MEM & J, two young DJs from Milan, had remixed my words over a disco bassline. They intended to satirize and mock my message, to turn my words against me. But something unexpected happened. The remix was too catchy, too danceable and, in its own way, too revolutionary to serve its intended purpose. Instead, it became wildly popular. Within weeks, it was playing in clubs across the country, with people dancing to it. It even earned a gold record, which (ironically) fulfilled my most secret childhood dream: to be a singer.

As I reflected on this unlikely turn of events, I thought of my Nonno Gianni and how proud he would have been of me. My grandfather was a Sicilian through and through, but he had his moments of tenderness and sharp wit. He had often made my sister, Arianna, and me compete in a family version of *X Factor*. His favorite request was always the same: *Parlami d'amore Mariù*, a song from the 1930s made famous by Vittorio De Sica. Unfortunately, Nonno Gianni was also the most demanding judge in the history of talent shows, so neither of us ever won the 5,000-lire prize that was up for grabs.

Nevertheless, that strange blend of political rally and dance music, complete with a viral dance routine, had made me popular—especially with Gen Z. What was meant to undermine my message had become a megaphone amplifying it. Suddenly, I was no longer just another dull politician; I was an unexpected pop phenomenon.

That song was what convinced me to write this book. I realized that too many people were talking about me and my ideas without truly knowing me. So, I decided to open up and write about what I believe in and how I got to where I am today, directly from me to you.

I can imagine the reviews: "Barely forty and Giorgia Meloni is already writing an autobiography? Power must have gone to her head." Or, "Giorgia Meloni thinks she's qualified to draft a manifesto for the Italian Right, but she still has a long way to go." Comments like these might have some merit. But let me be clear: this book is not a theoretical manifesto for the Italian Right. At most, it is the story of a life spent contributing to the growth of the movement, without hiding from its challenges. There are others more suitable to write our political manifesto. If I were ever to do so, I would need to take a page from the books of those who have spent their entire lives working on these matters. These pages, meanwhile, aren't really even an autobiography—not in the traditional sense. Autobiographies belong to those nearing the end of their journey, and I'm not planning on leaving this world any time soon.

This book is different: it is my effort to share who I am and what I believe in, here and now. It is for anyone with the patience to read it, and also for myself.

In a political landscape where the majority lie about who they are, I see support for the Brothers of Italy continue to grow, and I want to be truthful and earnest with people about who I really am. I want those who choose to vote for me, support me, or believe in me to do so fully informed, knowing me for me: as a human being, with merits and limits, strengths and myriad weaknesses. A person who believes in what she does and tries to do it as best she can. In Italy, we always talk about politicians as though they are a separate species, as if they had suddenly landed on Earth from another planet. But politicians are also simply Italians, just like everyone else. There are good ones and bad ones. The challenge lies in distinguishing between the two. And we can't recognize them or choose the right ones if they don't tell the truth. So, here is my truth, whether you like it or not.

Perhaps I started writing this book mostly for myself. I'm at a crossroads in my life—far enough along to make a difference, but still vulnerable to losing my way. I've always believed that the greatest challenge for anyone in politics is to leave their mark while remaining loyal to the sincerest part of their life—what first inspired them to go to the front line. In the end, we all face the same inescapable question: *Did I change the system, or did the system change me?* I want to document who I am today so I can look back in ten, twenty, maybe thirty years' time and hold myself accountable. But I also want this book to be a tool for those who believe in me and in the things I do and say. Let this be a weapon should I betray my ideas and promises. No deception, no tricks.

In a world where everyone is trying to be someone, my goal is to remain true to myself, whatever it takes. To do so, I need to be honest—with you and with myself—about who I really am.

I am Giorgia, and this is my story so far.

Little Women

I owe everything to my mother. A strong-willed, cultured woman, she concealed a fragile soul beneath the armor she wore to face her life.

I owe her my love of books, my curiosity, my pride, my resilience, my dedication to work, my sense of freedom, and my unwavering need to speak the truth. She taught me everything with her no-frills approach that alone could fill a book. Today, once and for all, in front of everyone, I wish to thank her. Because most importantly, I owe her my life. Of course, every child could say that about their mother—but with mine, these words are even more profound. In fact, my exact words should be: "I owe everything to my mother and to her alone." The truth is, I wasn't even supposed to be born. When she became pregnant, Anna was twenty-three, already had an eighteen-month-old daughter, and was in a struggling relationship with my father—and he already had his suitcase packed, one foot out the door. Theirs was a wounded family.

My mother was a stubborn and free spirit, yet she had almost let herself be convinced that it didn't make sense to bring another child into the world under these circumstances.

I remember when she told me this and how long it took for me to fully process it. At times, I've thought that silence might have been better, sparing me from that morbid need adults have to bare their soul. But eventually, I came to understand the immense struggle of a single mother who held the power of a High Court in her hands: she could choose to let life begin, or send it back into the void.

The story she told me is always the same. The morning she was scheduled to undergo the routine pre-abortion tests, still fasting from the night before, she began walking toward the clinic. As she reached the door, she stopped, hesitated, and asked herself: *Is this truly my choice—to give up on the chance to become a mother for a second time?* Her answer came instinctively: *No, I don't want to give up. I don't want an abortion. My daughter will have a sister.*

It was a spring morning, the air gentle and pure. She felt a deep sense of having made the right choice. All that remained was to solidify her decision somehow, in whatever way she could. . . . She noticed a café across the street and went inside. "Morning. A cappuccino and a croissant, please." With that, her fast was over, the lab tests abandoned, and the scheduled abortion averted.

I owe everything to that breakfast, to my mother, to her resolute decision against all the odds. . . . In the words of Oriana Fallaci, "Some months later, I was lolling victoriously in the sun."

There are so many things I never knew about my mother's early life. I never even asked her how her relationship with my father began, how it evolved, or why it fell apart. I never asked about her thoughts, dreams, or illusions during those complicated times. It was the infamous 1970s, a period fueled by youthful fervor soon overshadowed by the cynical, ruthless power and logic of opposite extremist ideals. There were clashes in the piazzas, people using wrenches to attack each other, and a grim succession of bodies on the streets. Yet, those are not the only things to define that decade. It was also a time of relentless drive to change everything, share everything, and debate everything—an ethos that feels enviable in today's age of disposable values. My mother lived through that era, having just emerged from adolescence. She had been a sympathizer—perhaps even a militant one at times—with the right-wing youth movement back then. But she shared little of this with me. I know that, at some point, she had become infatuated with an older man who had already charted his path in life. It's never easy to decipher someone else's loves. Over time, though, I began to suspect that my mother wasn't so much pursuing love as she was seeking an escape from a strict family environment that felt suffocating to her rebellious spirit.

Her parents embodied the meeting of two very different worlds. My grandfather was Sicilian to the core, his face etched with an unwavering sense of duty. My grandmother, on the other hand, was thoroughly Roman, controlling my mother's fiery temper with the discipline of a Prussian general. She had an authoritative frown that we grandchildren never experienced. That's often how it goes: human beings, unlike trees, tend to grow softer, not harder, as time passes, becoming as tender as sapling wood.

My grandparents, however, were not so tender with their daughter. To them, whatever she did was wrong. Admittedly, my mother was always a unique personality, but I'm not sure whether her rebellious nature provoked this strictness, or whether their lack of leniency is what made her a rebel. Toward the end of her life, I often debated this with my grandmother, pushing for the latter possibility. I never managed to change her mind.

My mother's yearning to leave her parents' home was so strong that, as soon as she reached adulthood, she began building her own family—one piece at a time, like assembling a structure with Lego bricks. One of those pieces (perhaps the most important one) was my father, an accountant from northern Rome—however, he was deeply flawed.

For instance, when my mother was discharged from the hospital after giving birth to me, he didn't even come to pick us up. Suffice it to say, he wasn't exactly the ideal partner.

When I was still very young, he decided to take off for the Canary Islands on a boat named *Cavallo Pazzo* (Crazy Horse). He set sail and vanished from our lives.

I don't remember the day he left. Frankly, I can't remember ever living with him.

I must have come to realize this bit by bit.

The awareness of a father who is no longer there, who vanishes into thin air, is something that's hard to explain. It may leave a deeper wound than a father's death. At least then you can imagine him looking down at you from heaven. But when he chooses to leave, you're left grappling with the ghost of a person who isn't there.

I think he lived with us for a few months in the upscale Roman neighborhood Camilluccia—the district of well-heeled Romans, reputed for their affluence and reserve. We stayed in that house for a while, even after he had left.

Two events from our time in that house left an indelible mark on my life. One felt straight out of a scene from the detective movies that were so popular at the time. The other was more like something from a Stephen King novel. Although I've always loved his stories, living through one is an entirely different matter.

We had two German shepherds, Ettore and Eva. Eva, as is often the case with bitches around newborn babies, became like a mother to us. She would sleep beneath the cradle and bark at anyone who approached—even my father, which gives you an idea of how perceptive she was.

As I mentioned, our neighborhood was rather upscale, and our neighbor was a political bigwig in those days.

One evening, perhaps due to some noise they'd heard, agents from the neighbor's security detail decided to conduct a routine check, sneaking into the garden outside our building. Alarmed, my mother ran outside shouting, "I'm armed!" She froze, terrified in the semidarkness, just as Ettore and Eva rushed out, barking furiously. Quite a commotion ensued, but the evening ended peacefully.

A few nights later, though, the same security detail returned to sweep the area. This time, Ettore and Eva leaped over the fence and went on the attack. Seeing the two huge German shepherds charging at them, the agents drew their weapons and shot, hitting Ettore in the leg.

Hurt and frightened, Ettore began digging under the fence to get away. Besides being injured in the leg when he was shot, in the struggle to get away he also lost his sight in one eye.

Ettore was a marvelous animal. Despite his handicap, he remained the same. He allowed us to do anything to him—he even loved it when we put skates on his paws. But at the slightest hint of an external threat, his wolflike instincts kicked in. I was twelve when he died, having spent every one of those years with him. Losing him was devastating, and he remains the animal I have loved most in my life.

That brings me to the second memory that left a lasting impression on me: the image of a large stuffed panda devoured by flames, its glass eyes staring hauntingly at me.

My sister, Arianna, and I loved to experiment. We once dismantled Barbie's house to convert it into an unlikely rocket ship. We'd set paper and small objects on fire just to observe how they crumpled or melted. We rearranged furniture to create elaborate sets for stories that we invented. We were a dynamic duo. Until my daughter, Ginevra, was born, my sister was the most important person in my life. There is no secret I keep from her, and no advice I haven't sought from her. Even now, with both of us leading such busy lives, I feel a void if we don't talk at least once a day. I use my phone so much for work that I have an aversion to phone calls, but my sister is the one person who I genuinely feel the physical need to call. And just as she did when we were little, she tells me stories to help me fall asleep. More than anyone else, she has the gift of giving me a sense of peace, making me feel at home, and bringing me joy. Time spent with her is as vital as the air I breathe. I will never be able to thank her enough for the love she has given me and for being a constant role model throughout my life. Arianna is, without a doubt, the best person I have ever met on this earth.

But back to the day our mother lost the house—and a few years off her life in the process. That day, my sister and I had one goal: to organize a nighttime party. We built a makeshift fort in our room, filling it with toys, dolls, snacks, and drinks. When we finished, we looked at each other. What was missing? Light. But it had to be a dim light, otherwise Mamma would know we were still awake. We eventually came up with a solution: a candle. It was Arianna who found it, but I was the one who lit it.

It was only four in the afternoon, so we had to wait for nightfall to have our party. To kill time, we went to another room to watch cartoons. We left the lit candle behind.

How much time went by? I'll never know. All I remember is that, in the middle of an episode of *Candy Candy*, we heard a deafening crash from our bedroom. The three of us—my sister, mother and I—ran to see what had happened. Opening the door, we were nearly engulfed by flames. There it was: the panda burning along with all our toys. The noise we'd heard was the shutter collapsing.

In no time at all, the fire consumed the entire apartment. We fled with nothing but a single bag hastily packed with pajamas, two pairs of pants, and a T-shirt. All of a sudden, we were out on the street, alone and homeless. My mother had to start from scratch. A gargantuan task. Looking back, I sometimes joke that this experience is what gave me the courage many years later to rebuild a political house of my own after ours had gone up in smoke. After all, I'd already seen it done when I was four—why couldn't I succeed at thirty-five?

After selling the apartment, now reduced to a charred shell, my mother bought another one near my grandparents in the Garbatella neighborhood. A working-class district with public housing just outside the Aurelian Walls, it's nestled like a tiny jewel between Via Ostiense and Via Cristoforo Colombo, and had developed in the 1920s under the tufa rock that looms over the Basilica of Saint Paul.

Garbatella is my neighborhood not just because it's where I grew up and lived for many years, but because we can never be indifferent to the place that shapes us. We are unique in the world precisely because of where we come from.

Though the area gained widespread attention thanks to (or perhaps no thanks to) the TV series *I Cesaroni*, the first person to talk about it in cinema was the filmmaker and actor Nanni Moretti, who claims it as his favorite neighborhood in the movie *Dear Diary*. And how right he was.

Today it is a sought-after area, offering the charm of a made-to-measure hamlet despite being near the heart of Rome. It's far removed from the metropolitan beehives built in the 1970s, products of a collectivist culture that treated humans like battery hens. However, I didn't live in that magical, secret part of Garbatella, but rather a few hundred yards away—in the more modern section near the Lazio regional government building. Yet even there, the sense of belonging was palpable. It felt like living in a village within the city.

As a child, my life was divided between school, the church community, and the small house where my grandparents lived. They were authority figures for my sister and me, offering daily guidance. They were still young, around fifty years old, and they cared for us like a second set of parents.

My Nonno Gianni always reminded me of the adventure writer Emilio Salgari. Although my grandfather had never traveled outside Italy, never flown on a plane, he loved weaving tales of adventure set in the most far-flung places—whether real or imagined. Born in Messina, Sicily, he had come to Rome after World War I to work at what was then the Ministry of the Military Navy. Nonno Gianni was endlessly fun, always finding ways to spark competition between my sister and me, crowning the loser as the "Regina della monnezza" (the queen of trash). He was the only true father figure we ever had, and he died when Arianna and I had just reached adulthood. To us, he was a man of great strength, though his health had been declining for years. Two heart attacks, followed by a stroke and then dialysis, took their toll. He often argued with my Nonna Maria, who would force him to drink quarts of water daily, as prescribed by his doctor. He was on a strict diet and smoking was forbidden—yet he couldn't resist sneaking out to indulge in *cotolette fritte*, fried veal cutlets.

When we were little, my sister and I were fortunate enough to know our great-grandmother, Nonna Nena, who lived to the age of ninety-two. Nonna Nena (whose real name was Maddalena) had endured the loss of her son Angelino, who had died of meningitis at the age of five and was widowed early in life, when her daughter (my Nonna Maria) was just twelve. Like so many others in the first half of the twentieth century, Nonna Nena had faced much bereavement and hardship. Her struggles led to her daughter (my grandmother) being sent to a convent school, where she received a strict and disciplined education—the stories of which were her favorite topic of conversation. Nonna Maria never forgot her little brother. Throughout her life, she brought flowers to the cemetery and would light a candle for him. When she no longer had the strength to go to the Verano Monumental Cemetery, she asked us to carry on the tradition. Now that she is no longer with us, we continue to honor her wishes.

My grandparents lived in an apartment building with designated homes for ministry employees. I still remember how proud my grandfather was when he finally paid off the mortgage. At last, that tiny home was all his. It was a two-room apartment, just under five hundred square feet, and it was where my mother had grown up. The kitchen doubled as the dining room, and it was the heart of our domestic life. No one living inside those walls ever saw a sofa. There was a single table, and that is where we ate, did our homework, played, or watched TV. My mother was always working, so my sister and I spent our afternoons after school in that all-purpose living room. There was a narrow hallway with a convertible bed that we slept in whenever our mother chose to go out for the evening, in an attempt to live her own life (as much as that was possible). As my grandmother would say, we were tucked in "one with her head on top, one with her feet on top." Which means that I spent many nights in a hallway with my sister's feet stuck in my face. When I grew older, I was finally rewarded: a cot in the kitchen, all to myself. It was a significant upgrade.

Nonna Maria was a homemaker, and she treated caring for the home like a mission, organized according to a meticulous schedule and following procedures to a tee. To clean a house that size, she'd start at dawn and work until dusk. Not even the dog was spared—he was locked in the bathroom while she did her chores, then had to suffer the indignity of having his teeth brushed with a toothbrush.

That small dog with his bright smile was a poodle named Charlie. My sister and I were in charge of taking him for a walk every afternoon for years, earning us the neighborhood nickname of "Charlie's owners."

Whenever I see the vast mountain of toys my daughter leaves strewn around the house, I think back to an old shoebox where I kept my favorite toy: building blocks. Today, my daughter has enough blocks to construct the third lane of Rome's Great Ring Road, whereas Arianna and I could barely re-create our grandmother's kitchen to scale with our blocks. I'm not sure which way of growing up is better. Or perhaps I do know, but I'm afraid to admit it.

Arianna and I were remarkably independent. We even traveled by plane alone as young as the ages of eight, nine, and ten years old, to spend a few weeks' vacation with our father in the Canary Islands. The flight attendants would tie red envelopes with the necessary documents around our necks, and we would board the plane that would take us to Madrid for a stopover. One time we were stranded because the airport staff member who was supposed to meet us never showed up. We found ourselves lost in the seemingly enormous terminal. While I was in a daze, Arianna took my hand and somehow got us onto the correct flight. I'll never understand how she managed it. Our parents argued bitterly about that misadventure.

* * *

It may be hard to believe, but until I was fourteen, I was quite introverted. As a child, I always wore a sullen expression—the same one I have today when I prepare to answer the journalist Lilli Gruber's questions. To anyone who mocks my brazen and grumpy demeanor, I can show them a kindergarten photo where I look exactly the same.

I've always been on the defensive. A friend of my mother recently told me I was the kind of child who couldn't tolerate fairy tales, disliked being teased, and observed adults with mistrust and a raised eyebrow. When asked, "What kind of kid were you?" the answer is always the same: "A serious one." That description still lingers in my mind today.

I had a difficult temperament, and making friends never came easily to me. I was a textbook Capricorn—not shy or distrustful, but fiercely and stubbornly protective of my personal space. In other words, I was not an exuberant child, something I see even more clearly now as I watch my daughter laughing, chatting, and befriending everyone she meets. I, on the other hand, spent most of my time with my sister and a small circle of others. At school, I would stand my ground when provoked. I remember snapping at a classmate who refused to talk to any kid who didn't have a father. Yes, I was prickly, quick to retort, and my looks certainly didn't help my social life.

My grandmother wasn't a trained nutritionist by any stretch. To give you a rough idea, she was the kind of person who believed that a bit of extra weight was a sign of good health. Every night, dinner included milk and cookies. As a result, by the time I was nine years old, I weighed over 140 pounds. It's official: my grandmother wrecked my metabolism. And yet, to the very end, whenever I visited her, she'd offered me a snack. "Come on," she'd say, "you're too skinny, eat something."

I always looked skinny to her, even when I was the size of a blimp. "You're too thin. Are you eating? What are you eating?" Whenever I traveled abroad, her biggest concern was always the same: "Be honest, what did they feed you?" During a two-week school trip to Berlin, my grandmother constantly called me to ask, "What are they feeding you there? Furstels? All they eat are furstels there!" (I think she meant to say "wurstel," sausages.)

Though I made fun of her for it, I knew it was a completely normal reaction for anyone who had experienced wartime hunger. It had shaped her obsession with full stomachs.

My mother was also a member of this "anti-beauty conspiracy." For practical reasons, she kept our hair short in that unflattering 1980s hairdo that looked like a banana boat. Not even Charlize Theron could pull off that look, let alone me. My oversized head earned me the nickname "capocciona," (big head) from my grandmother. You get the picture. I could pretend that my grandmother dubbed me that due to my great intelligence . . . but no, that wasn't the case. To make matters worse, they sent us out into the world wearing tracksuits. Unsurprisingly, I wasn't considered attractive. And children, as we all know, aren't exactly politically correct when it comes to teasing someone because they're fat, poorly dressed, or whose family situations aren't the norm.

My mother was constantly working, continually inventing different professions. At one point, she thought she could be a writer and ended up writing 140 romance stories. Her extraordinary intelligence made her eclectic, but she lacked the luck to make it work—there was just never enough money. It was an unfortunate combination of circumstances that led her to be absent-minded and forced limitations on our lives—and for a child, that can really leave its mark. I still remember one Fat Tuesday celebration at school when I was the only one without a mask. My teacher quickly fashioned a daisy mask out of paper for me. My sister didn't fare much better: our mother bought her a space pirate outfit that wasn't the ideal choice for a girl. Arianna loves to tell the story of the time when Nonna Maria was asked to contribute to a buffet for some party or other (I can't really remember which one now). She gave my sister 5,000 lire, and Arianna went to the café, bought five pastries, and arrived at the party with a small paper bag. Meanwhile, everyone else had brought trays heaving with goodies and homemade cakes. To save the day, the teachers took the five pastries and mixed them in with the food on one of the other trays. My sister was so traumatized by that day that now, whenever she organizes a party for her own children, she starts baking cakes like there's no tomorrow, preparing enough sandwiches to feed the whole school.

But let me be clear: we were happy children. Despite my occasional bad temper and my father's absence, I was never sad because I had a family that gave me all the love I needed. I say this because—although I defend the nuclear family and the sanctity of marriage—I believe that the state should incentivize the most solid form of union to protect the children. I have witnessed how, even in a family where one of the two parents is missing, it is possible to grow up perfectly happy, thanks to the selflessness of those who shoulder that responsibility.

Inside my family, I had everything I needed. It was outside that family circle that I did not find that same acceptance.

I have talked about this in Parliament, during a debate on the Zan draft law. This was proposed as a measure to protect homosexuals from discrimination, but it is actually a dangerous tool, conceived to impose gender doctrine from as early as elementary school.

Our parliamentary colleague, Alessandro Zan, backed the draft law because he had been bullied as a child for being homosexual. But I was bullied, too—and I'm heterosexual. Bullying, for all sorts of reasons, is a universal experience, to a greater or lesser extent. This is why it is almost impossible to resolve the matter by making a long list of specific hate crimes, as if one type of insult or humiliation is worse than another. The Italian constitution already condemns discrimination in all of its forms, be it sex, race, language, religion, political opinion, personal and social status. To my mind, this definition already covers everything, including homosexuality. Drawing up a more specific list means entering dangerous territory because it inevitably means excluding anyone not explicitly protected by specific laws. Doing so creates a precarious mechanism, leading to endless and problematic hierarchies. Is it worse to offend a woman or someone who is gay? Someone who is gay or black? Someone who is black or disabled? Discrimination is discrimination. Period. No form of discrimination is more or less serious than another.

I found being bullied extremely tough, but I must admit that it shaped me and drove me to change so I wouldn't be such an easy target.

I remember everything clearly. One day, I was at the beach, and I was in my bathing suit, of course. Some kids were playing volleyball, and I asked to join them, but was rebuffed as they shouted back at me: "No, fatso! You *can't* play!" And they threw the ball so hard it hit me in the face. In that moment, I wanted to die. But Arianna, as always, was at my side. Unlike me, she was popular, pretty, and fun. Despite being forced to drag around a lumpy potato (yours truly), she was happy to argue with anybody to defend me.

Now that time has passed, I'm grateful to those idiots—they were the first to teach me that enemies can be useful. They spur you on to overcome challenges, to push past your limits, and to correct your mistakes. Of course, Plutarch explains it much better when he says, "a sensible man will receive profit even from his enemies. . . . But since friendship has nowadays become very mealy-mouthed in freedom of speech, voluble in flattery and silent in rebuke, we can only hear the truth from our enemies." It's also thanks to those kids that I developed a resilient personality to tackle both hardships and fears. I decided to go on a diet and lost twenty-two pounds in three months. I was going to play volleyball, all right, that was for sure. And I did, before the end of the season.

I learned the hard way that healthy eating habits are crucial for young people, not just for their health but also for their social lives. Whether we are accepted has a lot to do with our bodies. Though it might seem superficial, it's just a fact.

During my tenure as Minister of Youth, I turned this personal insight into political action. I commissioned a study on the subject that revealed the shocking prevalence of eating disorders, with over 300,000 "ProAna" websites. These are communities and personal blogs that promote anorexia, where young people share tips on how to keep their parents from discovering they are fasting, and even how to avoid being hungry, spreading seriously unpleasant practices and self-harm. Yet, there were no resources widely available to challenge these disorders. Not a single website for families that tells you how to recognize the warning signs or who to turn to for help.

I credit my strong character with saving me from falling into the spiral of eating disorders. Until I was thirty years old, I didn't think to blame my father for my problems as a child, believing his abandonment had no impact on me. But eventually, I looked inward and realized I was lying to myself. And denying the truth is never good for you. You must always have the courage to face the truth, even when you're wrong. Of course, mistakes are inevitable, but you must be self-aware and take responsibility for them.

We now live in a society where some may lead you to believe you can shift blame onto others. But that's not how the world works. Each of us has a role to play, for better or worse. Italy will change only when we understand that we are all part of the whole. We must learn that we cannot fix Italy from the outside, as if we aren't a fundamental part of it. To quote Michael Jackson, if you want to change, start with the man in the mirror.

Everything I've done wrong in my life, everything that made me angry, that I didn't like or didn't understand . . . I strive to understand the reasons behind all these things. I need to be honest with myself if I truly want to know who I am.

For a long time, I refused to admit to myself that my relationship with my father was a problem. Then, while watching the silliest American romcom (*The Perks of Being a Wallflower*), I had an epiphany. In the movie, the main character blunders into a succession of humiliations and miserable men. There's endless weeping. She can't figure out why she gets hung up on men who are objectively terrible. Finally, her male friend tells her the eye-opening truth: "*We accept the love we think we deserve.*"

I realized that all that my father had done was deeply significant. It wasn't just his abandonment of our home—after all, many fathers still remain a part of their children's lives after a separation. No, what hurt the most was his indifference to us. His lack of love is what scarred me.

Which is exactly why, at the age of eleven, I decided I never wanted to see him again.

It was my own choice, but I must admit that he didn't seem especially bothered by it. Until then, we'd see him for a few weeks every summer. Then we broke off all contact for several years. After sailing around the world, my father settled on one of the tiniest islands in the Canaries, La Gomera. Measuring just 14 miles across, it features the primordial landscape that is typical of volcanic islands: black sandy beaches, alien rock formations, and a prehistoric forest. When my sister and I were little, we didn't appreciate just how beautiful the island was: we were too focused on our games and the near total freedom we had to roam around the place. All the islanders knew each other, and there was no mass tourism to speak of back then, so us kids could run around from dawn 'til dusk.

We lived in the capital, San Sebastián, and spent a lot of time in the big restaurant our father had opened there. I remember one terrifying incident when Arianna and I swam to the nearby rocks on a wild beach. As we swam, the tide rose, trapping us in the water and crushing us against the rocks. Escaping was a Herculean task and we emerged covered in cuts and bruises.

We were lively girls and our father tolerated our . . . shall we say, less than discreet antics. We often played pranks on him, and there were a few times we pushed him too far. Looking back, he was right to lose his temper. Once, we were sailing on a boat and my sister threw a huge rock into the water while I hid. She shouted to my father, "Papa, Papa! Giorgia's fallen into the water!" Terrified, he dove into the sea to look for me, nearly drowning . . . until I popped out of my hiding place, laughing hysterically with Arianna.

The last summer we visited, my father thought it was a good idea to leave for a week. He left us behind with his partner, who—understandably—wasn't jumping for joy at the prospect. When he returned, instead of apologizing to her or us, he gave us a talk that I have never forgotten. It was the death knell for our relationship. I don't wish to repeat his words, but suffice to say he made it clear we were not his priority when it came to love. He insisted we had to behave accordingly whenever we stayed with him.

That marked the end. Or perhaps, the real and final end was two years later when he sent me a telegram for my thirteenth birthday. It was signed *Happy birthday. Franco.* "Papa" was evidently too personal.

The constant need to meet high standards, especially in male-dominated environments, along with my fear of disappointing those who believe in me, likely stem from the lack of my father's love.

I grew up convinced that I didn't deserve anything. My reaction was to strive relentlessly to prove otherwise. Because it boils down to this: what happens is one thing, and how we deal with it is another. And how we deal with it makes all the difference. Life is less what happens to us because of someone else's actions, and more about how we choose to react. Our courage to face up to situations defines us. In short, I discovered I was an unwitting stoicist.

Each day, I grapple with fear—fear of inadequacy, of falling short in the eyes of others. But this fear is also my strength; it drives me to keep studying and learning, to strive for the highest marks in every subject, even when I'm starting from scratch. This fear fuels my attention to detail, my stubbornness, my commitment, my willingness to make sacrifices. Competing with men (not with women), seeking their approval, friendship, and the esteem of my fellow fighters who are now my fellow party members, of all the men I respect and have met throughout my life . . . all of it is the result of that wound.

If this is who I am today, it is thanks to my father—for better or worse.

When he died a few years ago, I felt nothing. Writing those words is still painful. When I heard the news, I was furious that I felt nothing. I realized then just how deep the black hole was that I had buried my pain in—the pain of not being loved enough.